The Traditions of Glastonbury

E. RAYMOND CAPT M.A., A.I.A., F.S.A. Scot.
Archaeological Institute of America

1987 EDITION WITH INDEX

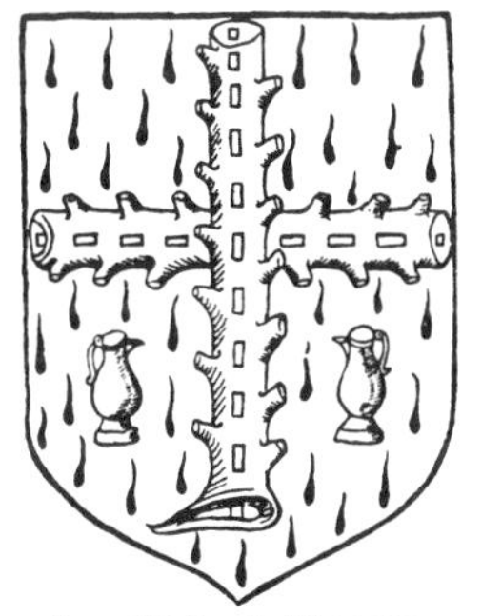

Arms of St Joseph of Arimathea

PUBLISHER
ARTISAN PUBLISHERS
P.O. Box 1529
Muskogee, Oklahoma 74402
(918) 682-8341
www.artisanpublishers.com

ISBN 0-934666-10-5
Library of Congress catalog card number: 82-072525

Cover design taken from this Banner of the
Parish Church of Pilton, Somerset, England.

PREFACE

One day a small boat, from one of the large merchant ships anchored in the Bristol Channel, tied up at the causeway of the Lake Village. A bearded man and a slim young boy in his early teens stepped ashore. They were no strangers to the villagers who crowded around to welcome them. The merchant had been coming by their village for many years, on his way to the lead mines of the Mendip Hills. It was known that he held a very important position in the powerful Roman government and carried the title "Nobilus Decurio." It was rumored that he owned many of the merchant ships that came to these Isles of the West, from Rome and Phoenicia, to barter for metal and other goods.

The auburn haired lad was also known. He had accompanied his uncle on a prior visit, staying at the village and exploring the surrounding territory, while His uncle conducted his business at the nearby Mendip lead mines. But this time a woman, perhaps in her early thirties, was with them. As the boy helped the woman ashore, the crew proceeded to unload various sized chests and sacks, obviously belonging to them. Accommodations were soon found and the baggage was carried to one of the tiny huts facing the estuary.

In the weeks that followed, the merchant and the boy constructed a wattle hut, similar to those of the village, on a nearby island. The site they chose was at the base of a hill from which ran a spring of fresh water. Hawthorne and oak trees dotted the landscape. Small game and fish were in abundance and the marshy fertile shores promised bountiful crops. When the hut was finished, the woman and the boy moved from the village to their new home. The merchant and his men sailed away.

Glastonbury Tor.

Jesus and His mother, Mary were alone ...

Painting by V. J. Lee.

RECONSTRUCTED GLASTONBURY LAKE VILLAGE MUD AND WATTLE HUT SUCH AS OUR LORD WOULD HAVE OCCUPIED.

INTRODUCTION

The Bible is strangely silent concerning Jesus' movements between the ages of 12 and 30. The only incident of childhood recorded in the Gospels is His visit to the Temple at about the age of twelve. The occasion was the Feast of the Passover, when lectures were given in the Temple of Herod. There in the audience, listening to the words of the learned Rabbis, was the boy Jesus. Occasionally, as was His privilege, He asked a few questions. Then, He dared to disagree with the speakers. Soon, Jesus was invited to come to the lecture platform where He could be better seen and heard. As the debate progressed, the learned teachers were astonished and mystified at the questions the boy could propound and then answer Himself. The Rabbis wondered about this boy who could confound and amaze the world famous Faculty of the University of Palestine.

The last New Testament account of the boy Jesus is found in Luke 2:52, *"And Jesus increased in wisdom and stature, and in favour with God and man."* Then, eighteen years pass during which time the Scriptures are absolutely silent concerning the whereabouts and activities of the Divine Teenager. It has been the popular tradition for centuries that He lived in the village of Nazareth, Galilee, working as a carpenter until He took up His Galilean Ministry, at the age of thirty. Although the Gospels offer no record of these so-called "silent years," they do contain several distinct implications that these eighteen years were not spent in Palestine.

Consider the passage, *"And he came to Nazareth, where he had been brought up ... and the eyes of all them that were in the synagogue were fastened on him ... And they said, Is not this Joseph's son?"* (Luke 4:16-22) Two things strike us here. The usage of the expression, *"where he had been brought up,"* implies that while Jesus had spent His childhood in Nazareth He had not continued to live there. His more recent days had been spent elsewhere. This impression is strengthened by the fact that His hearers ask the question, *"Is not this Joseph's son?,"* almost as though they were in doubt as to His identity.

We also read that they asked, *"Is not this the carpenter's son? is not his mother called Mary? and his brethren, James, and Joses, and Simon, and Judas? And his sisters, are they not all with us? Whence then hath this man all these things?"* (Matt. 14:55, 56) Was Jesus such a stranger to them that the people could not refer to Him by name, but only by His relationship to the other members of His family whose identity was not in doubt?

Now, notice another passage of Scripture. *"And when they were come to Capernaum, they that received tribute money came to Peter, and said, Doth not your Master pay tribute? He saith, Yes."* (Matt. 17:24, 25) Now, we know that Jesus spent much of His time ministering in Capernaum. In fact, by comparing the account of the healing of the man sick with palsy as recorded in Matthew 9:1 with that of Mark 2:1, we find that Capernaum is described as His "own city." Yet, here was an enquiry being made about Jesus' liability to the 'strangers tax' (Roman poll-tax) which was levied on foreign visitors to Capernaum Most often, these were traders and merchants who conducted their business there. Evidently, Jesus must have been considered a 'stranger' by the custom officers of the city who should have known Him all His life.

Some Bible scholars have held that the tax in question was the Temple tax. However, unless the authorities were uncertain as to Jesus' nationality, which they surely were not, there could have been no doubt that Jesus was liable to pay the Temple tax. Moreover, the Temple tax would have been paid with a Jewish skekel, a coin especially minted for that purpose, whereas it was a Greek coin (stater) which Jesus provided. However one looks at this incident, there is more than a suggestion that Jesus had been absent from Palestine for some considerable time.

ANTIOCH STATER OF AUGUSTUS 27 B.C. - 14 A.D.

Consider this Bible incident: When Jesus appears upon the banks of the Jordan River where John was baptizing, the Baptist seems scarcely to recognize Jesus, even though they were first cousins and must have known each other during their early childhood. Finally, John recognizes who the stranger is and exclaims: *"Behold the Lamb of God!"* Now, if Jesus had been living in Nazareth all those years surely John would not have appeared puzzled as to His identity. Then, later, John sent two of his disciples to make a peculiar query: *"Are you he who should come or look we for another?"* Apparently, the two had not met for years since John displays a profoundly imperfect knowledge of the One whom he was proclaiming.

Yet another Bible incident, suggestive of Jesus' absence from His homeland is found in the story of Nathaniel. In the first chapter of the Gospel of John, verses 45-48: *"Philip findeth Nathaniel, and saith unto him, We have found him, of whom Moses in the law, and the prophets, did write, Jesus of Nazareth, the son of Joseph. And Nathanael said unto him, Can there any good thing come out of Nazareth? Philip saith unto him, Come and see. Jesus saw Nathanael coming to him, and saith of him, Behold an Israelite indeed, in whom is no guile! Nathanael saith unto him, Whence knowest thou me? Jesus answered and said unto him, Before that Philip called thee, when thou wast under the fig tree, I saw thee."*

Now, the facts are clear that Nathanael lived in Cana of Galilee, which is located about five miles from the city of Nazareth. If Christ had lived so close to him for eighteen years, it seems strange that Nathanael would not have known Him. Nathanael should have been acquainted with Jesus' command of the Scriptures and His Divine character. Would the very Son of God have no effect for eighteen years upon the community in which He dwelt?

In the light of these implications, the question could be asked: If Jesus was absent from Palestine then is there any evidence as to where He was during the eighteen years prior to beginning His ministry at the age of thirty? The answer is YES! Legends exist that Jesus traveled far and wide. The religious teachers of India assert He had dwelt among them studying there for three years before traveling on to what is now Tibet. Ancient religious books of India record Jesus visiting the Himalayan kingdom of Nepal. Other traditions take Jesus to Egypt. While it is possible that Jesus as an adult did visit other countries, the strongest and most persistent traditions place the teenage Jesus on the mystical Isle of Avalon, the little Somerset county town of Glastonbury, England.

It is not difficult to believe that Jesus, having previously visited the area with His uncle Joseph, would have remembered the beauty and quiet of the Isle of Avalon as a retreat in which to spend some years in study, prayer and meditation before His Ministry and Passion. The rich moist soil was favorable for cultivation and a copious supply of water gushed forth from the spring. Today this well is known as the "Chalice Well" or "Holy Well." Having been brought up as a child in the home of a carpenter, it would have been natural for Him to construct a home for His mother and Himself.

If one wonders why the selection of Glastonbury as the place for retreat and study by Jesus, there are two possible answers: (1) Here was an island unconquered by the Romans and remote from Roman influences and authority. Several attempts to conquer this area proved abortive. Julius Caesar, in a half-hearted manner, invaded Britain in 55 B.C., but did not progress into western Britain. It was not until A.D.

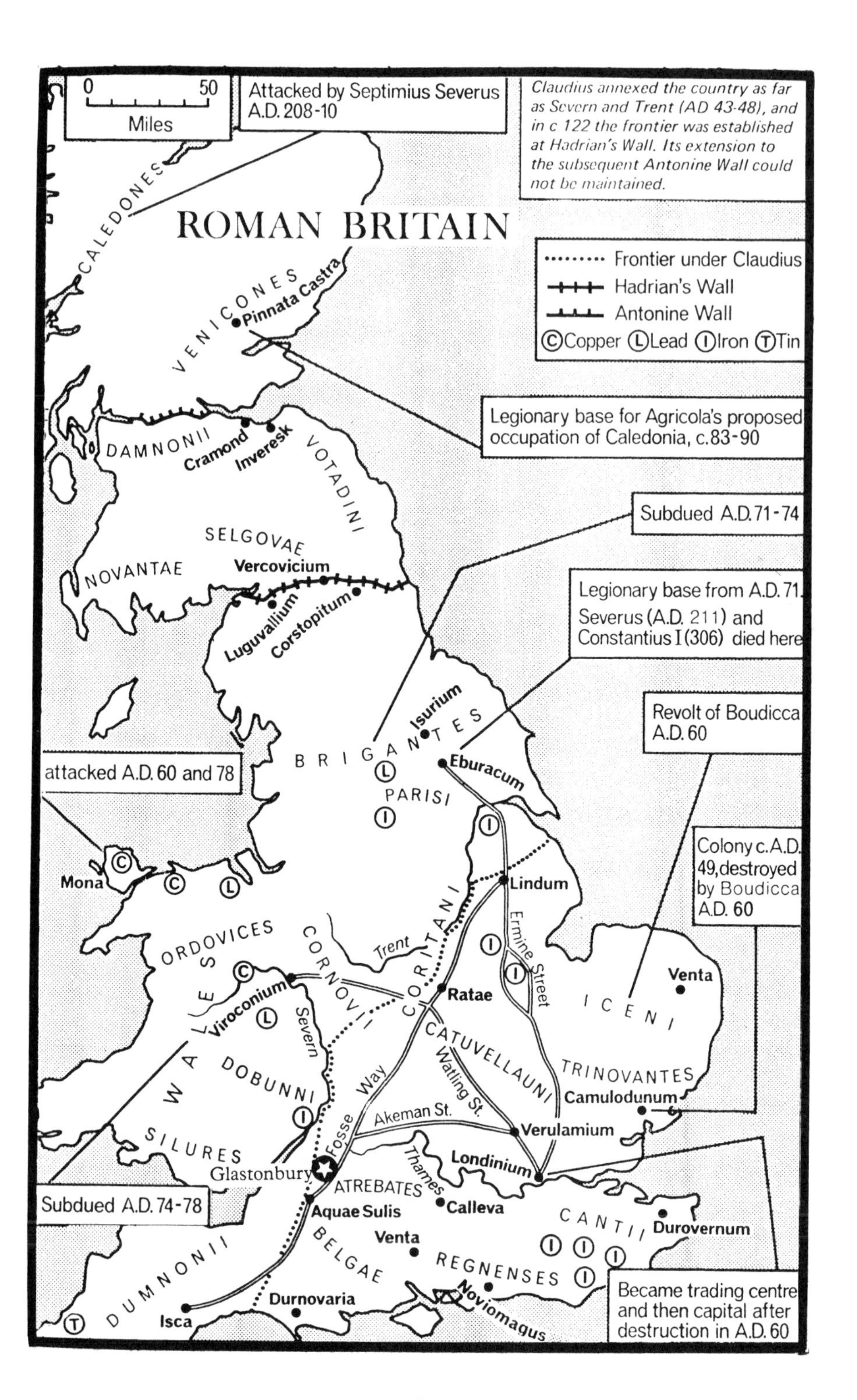
0 50
Miles
Attacked by Septimius Severus A.D. 208-10
Claudius annexed the country as far as Severn and Trent (AD 43-48), and in c 122 the frontier was established at Hadrian's Wall. Its extension to the subsequent Antonine Wall could not be maintained.
ROMAN BRITAIN
Frontier under Claudius
Hadrian's Wall
Antonine Wall
Copper Lead Iron Tin
CALEDONES
VENICONES
Pinnata Castra
Legionary base for Agricola's proposed occupation of Caledonia, c.83-90
DAMNONII
Cramond
Inveresk
VOTADINI
Subdued A.D. 71-74
SELGOVAE
NOVANTAE
Vercovicium
Luguvallium
Corstopitum
Legionary base from A.D. 71. Severus (A.D. 211) and Constantius I (306) died here
Isurium
BRIGANTES
Eburacum
Revolt of Boudicca A.D. 60
attacked A.D. 60 and 78
PARISI
Mona
Lindum
Colony c. A.D. 49, destroyed by Boudicca A.D. 60
CORITANI
Trent
Ermine Street
ORDOVICES
CORNOVII
Venta
Ratae
ICENI
Viroconium
WALES
Severn
CATUVELLAUNI
Watling St.
TRINOVANTES
DOBUNNI
Fosse Way
Camulodunum
Akeman St.
Verulamium
SILURES
Thames
Londinium
Glastonbury
ATREBATES
Subdued A.D. 74-78
Aquae Sulis
Calleva
CANTII
Durovernum
Venta
BELGAE
REGNENSES
DUMNONII
Noviomagus
Became trading centre and then capital after destruction in A.D. 60
Durnovaria
Isca

43 that the Romans began the conquest of Britain in earnest. By A.D. 47 their armies did reach Somerset, but stopped short of Glastonbury. (2) Glastonbury was the center of the Druidic faith in Britain. It was surrounded by the chief centers, such as Caerleon, Salisbury, Bristol, Bath, and Dorchester. Druidism was regarded by the Romans as its greatest religious opponent because of its widespread influence definitely opposed to Roman and Greek mythology.

There is little doubt but that the Roman invasions under Julius Caesar, and later under Claudius, were largely influenced by a desire to exterminate a cult which had for so long proved the rival of Roman civilization. In A.D. 61 Suetonius Paulinus, the legate in Britain, proceeded to carry out instructions received from Rome to extirpate Druidism at any cost. (Tacitus, Annals, XIV, Chap XXX) The powerful resistance offered by the native tribes to the Roman invasions was mainly due to the exalted doctrine of the indestructibility of the soul taught by their religion.

Druidism taught "Three duties of every man: Worship God, be just to all men, die for your country." Julius Caesar wrote: "The Druids teach that by none other way than the ransoming of man's life by the life of man is reconciliation with the Divine Justice of the Immortal Gods possible." (Comment, Lib. V) The basic Druid belief was in a Trinity, but not polytheism. The God-head was called "Duw," (the one without darkness who pervaded the universe.)

The emblem of Druidism was three golden rays of light, representing the three aspects, or persons, of the Trinity, emanating from the God-head. They were known as "Beli," the Creator as regards the past; "Taran," the controlling providence of the present and "Yesu," the coming Saviour of the future. Druidism thus anticipated Christianity and pointed to the coming Saviour under the very name by which Christ was called.

In Druidic Britain, Jesus would live among people dominated by the highest and purest ideals; the very ideals He had come to proclaim. What better place to reside than in a land prepared to receive His truth? When Joseph of Arimathea subsequently came back to proclaim the Saviour under the very name familiar to every Druid, no wonder he received a welcome at the hands of the Druids and a king whose religion was Druidism, or at least, sympathetic to their ideals. Druidism prepared the way for Christianity by its solid acceptance of "The Way." But for Druidism, Christianity might never have flourished. Druidism nourished it through all its early stresses, giving it the vigour to endure through adversity.

We may also think of Jesus as living a somewhat secluded life, doing kindly acts, but not performing any miracles, since we read that the wedding at Cana of Galilee was the occasion of His first miracle. Jesus' hidden years were undoubtedly years of preparation. They would have been spent in relative obscurity. There would have been nothing spectacular about Him to draw attention to Him. Traveling from His home, perhaps He visited various parts of the country, teaching the same principles as the "Sermon of the Mount," later preached in His Ministry in Palestine.

Jesus would confirm and enlarge the Druid's faith in the One God, with three aspects (the Trinity) and their belief in a coming "Yesu" or "Hesus." One thing is certain — Jesus never revealed His identity as the "Yesu" they expected. He had not, as yet, accomplished the redemption of His people and the salvation of Mankind. Finally, the day came for Him and His mother Mary to leave their island home. Before Jesus left, His Lake Village friends probably gathered to bid Him farewell. Perhaps they discussed what He had taught them and no doubt, after His departure, came to reverence the memory of the One whom they came to regard as a Holy Man. But, little did they know that He was the Saviour of the world and the "Hesus" of their Druidic faith.

They preserved His dwelling as a "sacred spot." Later, when Jesus' uncle Joseph of Arimathea (the Nobilus Decurio) and his companions returned to settle there after the Passion of Christ, they found that dwelling, the "Home of God" still standing. Only this could explain the two mysterious titles, which in the earliest times, clung to Glastonbury — "Secretum Domini" (The Secret of the Lord) and "Domus Dei." (The House of God)

We do not know how many times Jesus, as a grown man, may have taken extended voyages with His uncle Joseph, or to what other foreign countries He may have traveled. Perhaps, Mary, after their departure from Glastonbury, returned directly to Palestine and Jesus continued His travels. In any event, Jesus (at the age of thirty) did return to His Birthplace sometime in A.D. 29, because that was the year of His baptism by John in the River Jordan. This baptism began His ministry — thus ending His "silent" years.

GLASTONBURY

Glastonbury lies in the heart of Somerset County, in southwest England. In early British times, Glastonbury was an island at the back of a large oozy estuary, (the Uxella) covered by the waters from the Bristol Channel and drained by the rivers Axe, Parret and the Brue. The River Brue formed a navigable river as it wound its way from the foot of the nearby Mendip Hills (north of the town of Glastonbury) to the sea, just south of Bristol.

Dominating the landscape is the Glastonbury Tor, or mount, rising some 500 feet once a place of Druid worship. Excavations have revealed there was a dark-age settlement on the mount. Imported Mediterranean pottery of the sixth century was found among traces of wooden buildings and evidence of metal working. The highly defensive nature of the site suggests that this may have been the chief strong-bold (at Glastonbury) of one Melwas, king of the "Aestive Regio" (the Summer Kingdom) of Somerset. Perhaps the Tor stronghold was the political center of a much wider area than Glastonbury.

During the eight and ninth centuries, A.D., several small monastic communities were established on the Tor. Excavators found several tiny huts cut into the rock and a possible wooden church. Later a Norman stone church dedicated to St. Michael, the Archangel, was built on the highest part of the hill. This memorial was destroyed in the earthquake that shook Glastonbury in A.D. 1275. All that remains today of the church is a single tower, standing gaunt upon its desolate hill.

THE TOR

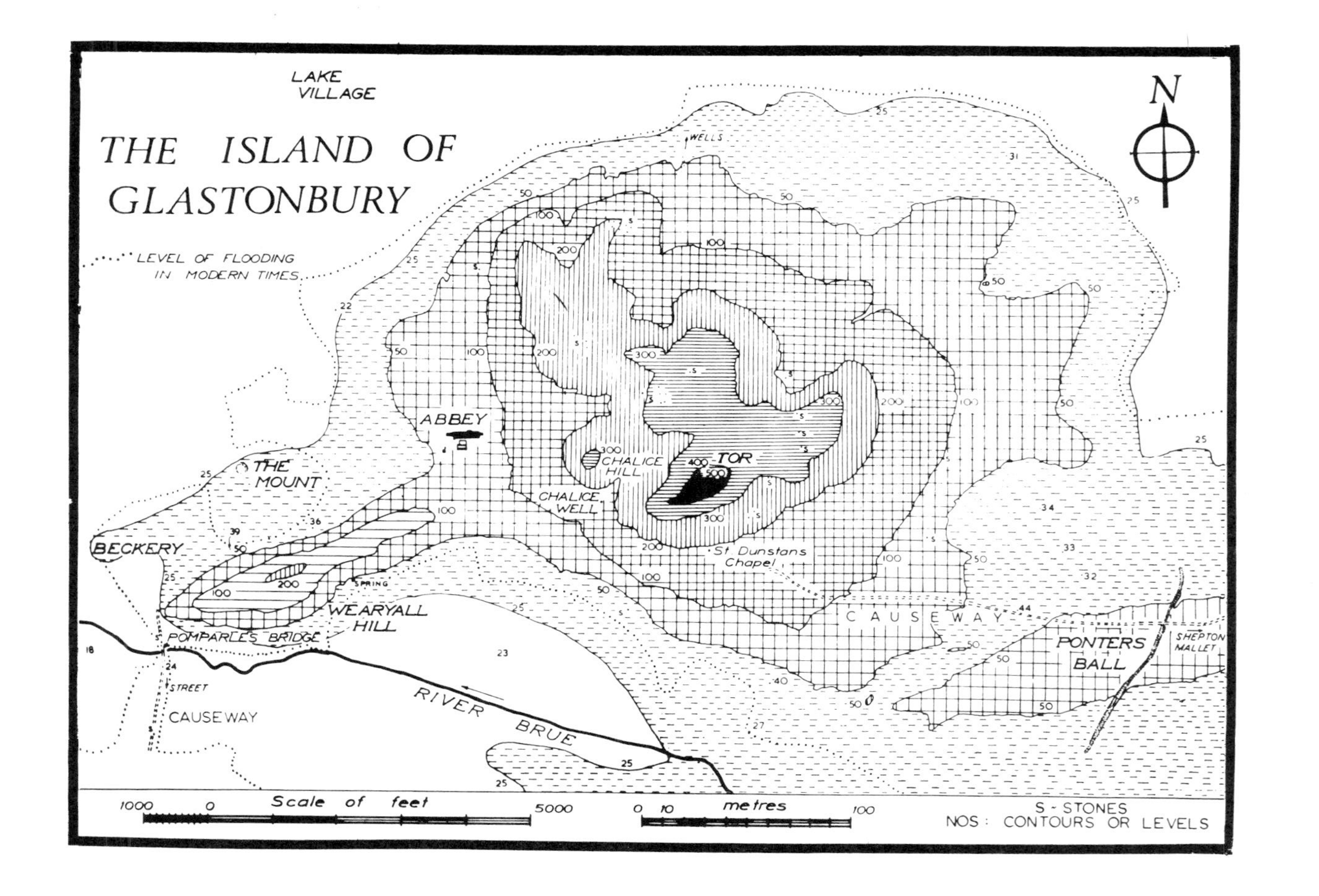
LAKE VILLAGE
THE ISLAND OF GLASTONBURY
N
LEVEL OF FLOODING IN MODERN TIMES
WELLS
ABBEY
THE MOUNT
BECKERY
CHALICE HILL
CHALICE WELL
TOR
St Dunstans Chapel
WEARYALL HILL
SPRING
POMPARLES BRIDGE
STREET
CAUSEWAY
RIVER BRUE
CAUSEWAY
PONTERS BALL
SHEPTON MALLET
1000 0 Scale of feet 5000
0 10 metres 100
S - STONES
NOS : CONTOURS OR LEVELS

The earliest name of Glastonbury was "Ynis-witrin" (Ynys gyrdyn - British ; Glaestingabyrig - Anglo-Saxon) or the "Glassy Island." Later, when it was found to be fruitful and ideal for the cultivation of apples, it was called "Insula Avalonia," or Isle of the Apple trees. Aval, in Welsh, means apple. Just how this area came to be known by the name "Glastonbury" remains in doubt. One suggestion is that the origin of Glastonbury is in "Glaestingaburgh", the hill fort of the Flaestings, a family who settled in the area. Another, and more accepted theory is that the Celtic word for green is "Glas" and hill is "ton." Glaston is therefore "the green hill," so named after the tor, or mount that dominates the landscape.

When the Saxons occupied Somerset, in the sixth century A.D., they built a town about half mile from the "green hill" and obtained a charter, adding "borough" or "bury" to the original name which has since remained "Glastonbury." The town of Glastonbury suffered incursions of the Danes in the ninth century. Later in A.D. 1184, a terrible fire destroyed part of the town and the Abbey. In A.D. 1276, an earthquake rocked the area and destroyed St. Michael's Church on the Tor and severely damaged the town.

Today, Glastonbury is a municipal borough, its charter of incorporation dating from A.D. 1705. The high road to the West, from London, passes, through Bath, Wells and Glastonbury. Its ruined Abbey is visited annually by the thousands of pilgrims who are drawn to its haunted vale, hallowed by the holy, half-forgotten lives and reverent worship offered here from most ancient times.

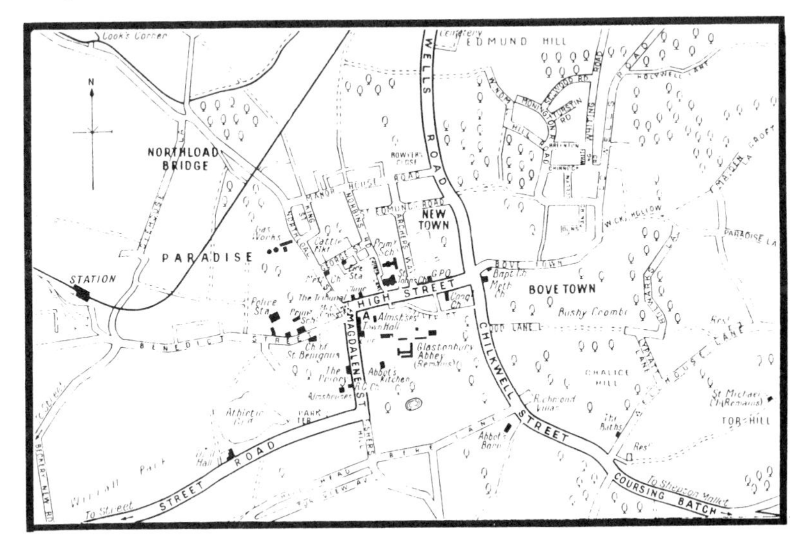

GLASTONBURY STREET PLAN

Although the swampy lake that surrounded the Isle of Avalon is today a grassy plain, having filled in with layers of peat, alluvial clays and gravels, many signs of the olden days still exist. Six meres (lakes) that were formed as the estuary retreated to the sea, existed as late as the early part of the 16th century A.D. Their names still show as fields on the survey maps of Somerset. One of the largest, recorded in A.D. 1540 as having been five miles in circumference, no longer exists. But, the pasture fields occupying part of the site are locally known as "Meare Pool."

In prehistoric times, village communities flourished on the shores and the many islands that dotted this tidal-swamp between Glastonbury and the sea. These village communities were inhabited by people of Celto-British (Cimmerian) origin. They lived in huts of mud and wattle, (a woven work of sticks interwined with twigs or branches) thatched with reeds. The huts were more or less circular and contained stone or clay hearths in the center. Often, the huts were washed with lime and had wood-work of willow, alder, beech and oak.

RECONSTRUCTION OF GLASTONBURY LAKE VILLAGE HUT

Perhaps for the sake of greater security, some of the villages were built in the shallow waters of large freshwater lakes. These were not far from the higher ground on which they grew their crops and grazed their sheep and cattle. Three such communities were found near Glastonbury, erected or built-up of platforms of stones, clay, brushwood and peat. From each community, wooden trackways ran to the mainland and nearby islands. These causeways consisted of two rows of pilings driven into the marsh and filled in between with layers of timbers, stone and peat. Excavations of the sites of these "lake villages" have provided a surprising amount of information about the inhabitants. The most noted of these excavations was at the "Glastonbury Lake Village."

The site of this village lies a little more than a mile from the center of the present town of Glastonbury. Archaeological excavations found that the village covered an area of three to four acres and consisted of about ninety huts varying from 20 to 30 feet in diameter. They were circular in shape, with a baked clay or stone slabbed hearth in the center. The platforms, for the huts, consisted of large timber logs covered with brushwood, rubble and reeds, with morticed beams binding the whole together. The walls were constructed of wattle and daub, that is, mats of woven sticks covered with clay. A layer of clay, covered with split wooden floor-boards, formed the floor of the huts. There was no palisade of timbers round this village as was found in the case of two older lake villages located at Meare and Godney.

Glastonbury Lake Village was constructed in or about 50 B.C. and remained inhabited until about A.D. 80, when it appears to have suffered destruction by fire. (perhaps by the Belgae tribes from the north) Therefore, it was in existence and inhabited during the life of Jesus of Nazareth. Its inhabitants were highly cultured, and skillful in various kinds of work. Among the tools found were knives, billhooks, sickles, saws, files, awls, bolts, gouges, adzes, keys, latchlifters, and harnesses—a truly remarkable array of equipment for a workman of those days.

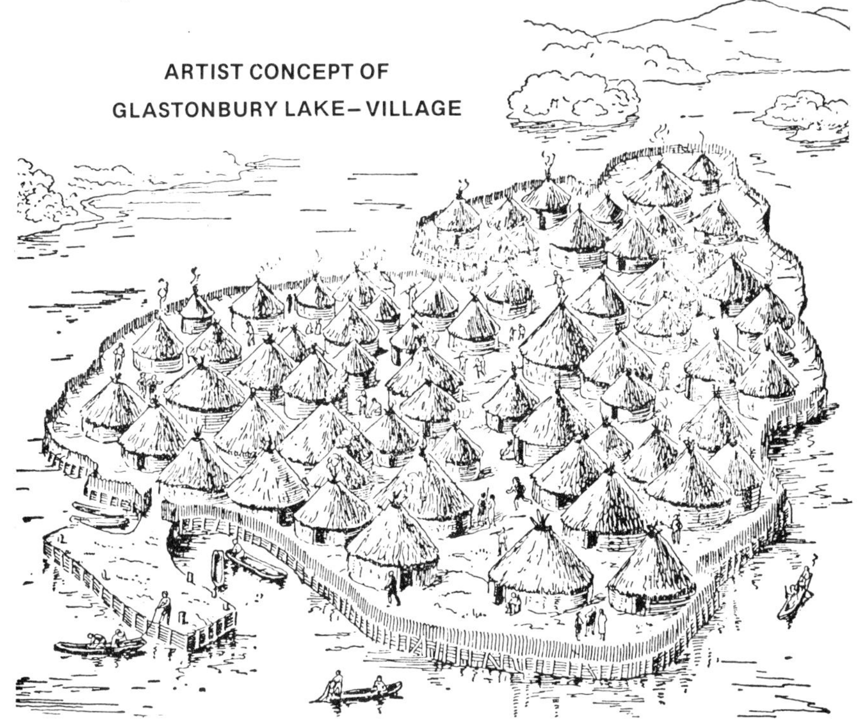
ARTIST CONCEPT OF
GLASTONBURY LAKE—VILLAGE

The men of Glastonbury were obviously expert carpenters. They made dug-out canoes over twenty feet long that enabled them to make long coastal trading voyages up and down the shores of the Bristol Channel and even across the rough stretch of water to the South Wales Coast. They constructed wheeled carts for transporting their crops and other loads by land. The wheels were nearly three feet across with twelve spokes skillfully fitted into a strong wooden axle-box. Their iron tools were well-balanced, with shapely wooden handles. They created perfectly-turned wooden bowls, artfully decorated in incised abstract patterns; a craft that survives unchanged in Wales today.

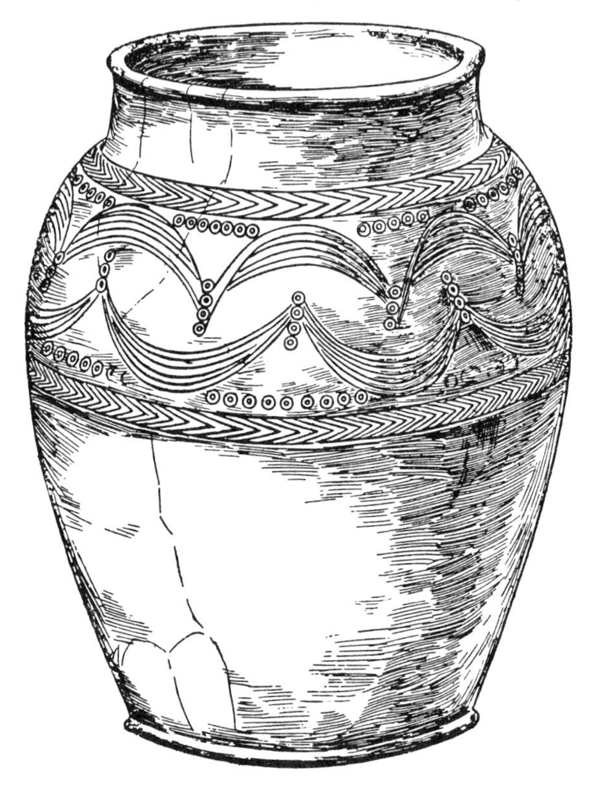

POTTERY FROM GLASTONBURY LAKE–VILLAGE

The lake-villagers produced wheel-made pottery, decorated in the characteristic flowing style of Late Celtic (La Tene) abstract art. Their skilled glass workers produced clear glass beads decorated with inlaid colored patterns. They even mastered the difficult art of enameling. They worked lead, from the Mendips, into a variety of utensils and worked both tin and copper into small ornaments. Combining tin and copper, they produced some of the finest examples of bronze artifacts of the Late Cetic Period. They can hardly be distinguished from similar hand-made implements fashioned by modern day country blacksmiths.

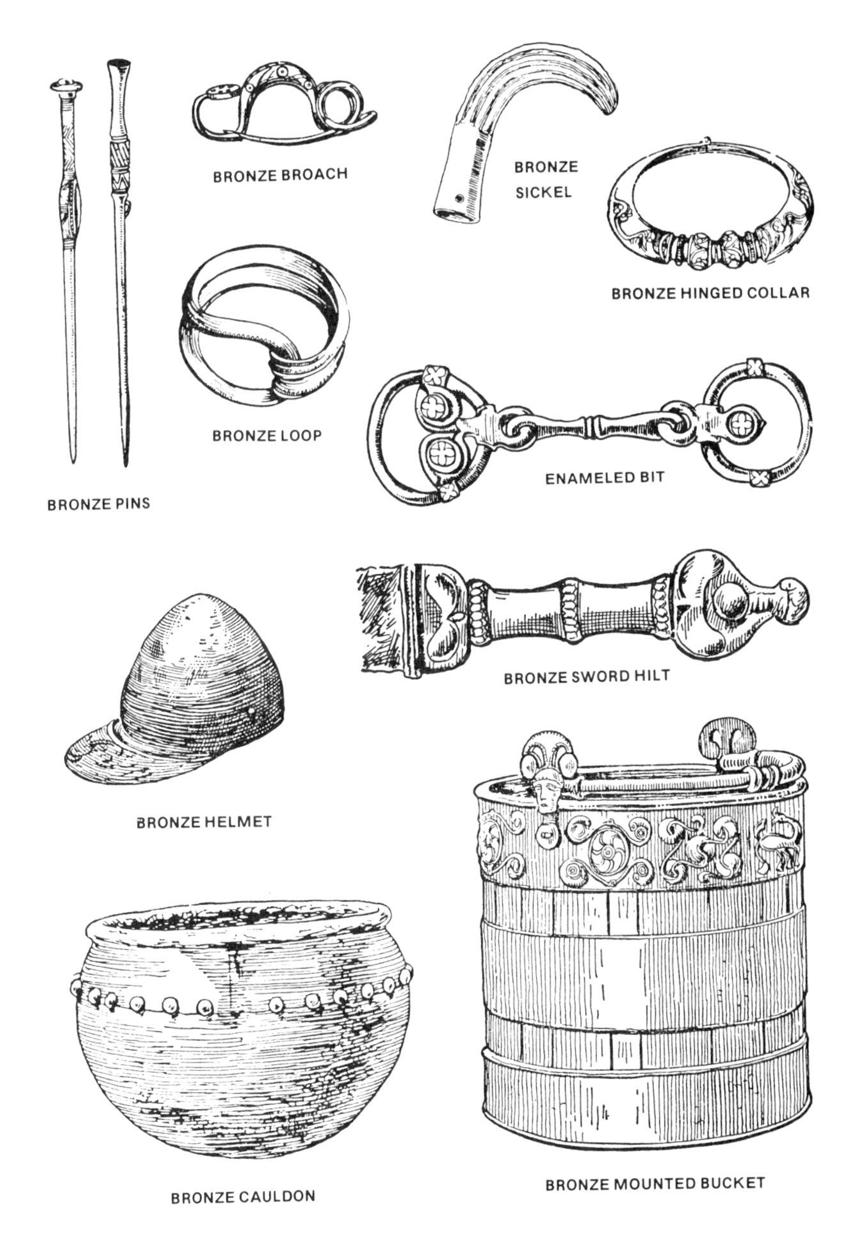

For basic subsistence, the villagers relied on a systematic and well-developed husbandry, growing wheat, barley, peas and beans while collecting blackberries and edible seeds in season. They stored their grain in circular pits (eight to ten feet deep and from three to five feet across) lined with plaited straw of reeds. They raised herds of short-horned cattle, large-horned sheep, pigs, goats, and horses. They gathered wild honey and fished with weighted nets and spears for perch, shad, trout, pike and salmon. They hunted the deer, otter, beaver, and the wild cat.

Perhaps it was the lead and copper from the nearby Mendip Hills that played an important role in the prosperity of the lake villages. The River Brue that wound its way from the village of Pilton, at the foot of the Mendips, through the estuary, by the lake villages ended in the Bristol Channel, the passage way for trading boats. Metal mined in the Mendips was brought down from the hills on wooden sleds to Pilton. From there it was loaded abroad small boats to be floated down to the Channel. (In those early days, the River Brue was about nine feet deeper that it is now) The lake villages of Glastonbury would have been a natural stop-over for trading. Bronze bowls and mirrors as well as glass beads and pottery, made at Glastonbury, have been found in other parts of Britain and Ireland.

BRONZE BOWL FROM GLASTONBURY LAKE-VILLAGE

Glastonbury communities enjoyed their peace and prosperity in an age of ever-growing violence and strife. They undoubtedly possessed the most advanced civilization of their time in Britain. It is this period of time and place that provides the setting of our "Preface" – a created story — based on the earliest of the ancient traditions relating to the beginning of Jesus' missing years — years centering around the figure of St. Joseph of Arimathea.

JOSEPH OF ARIMATHEA

To most Bible Scholars, Joseph of Arimathea is passingly remembered as the rich man who took the body of Christ from the cross and placed it in his private sepulchre (John 19:39-42) then passing silently out of the Scriptural picture soon after the Ascension of Christ.

The Bible indicates that Joseph, in addition to being rich, was a *"good man and a just"* man; a disciple of Jesus and a man of social distinction and official rank, for he was *"an honourable counsellor."* (Luke 23:50) He was evidently a member of the Sanhendrin, for we are told that he *"had not consented to the counsel and deed of them."* (Luke 23:51)

Joseph is always spoken of as belonging to Arimathea, which implies that it was his place of residence. Bible authorities identify this place with "Ramah," or "Ramallah," as it is called today. It was the birthplace of the prophet Samuel and is called, in the Septuagint, "Arimathaim." Being a member of the Sanhedrin, Joseph no doubt also had a residence in Jerusalem.

Ancient traditions, in the Eastern Church, assert that Joseph was the great-uncle of Jesus. This is confirmed by the Jewish Talmud which has Joseph as the younger brother of the father of Mary and thus was her uncle and a great-uncle to Jesus. The Harlein Manuscripts (in the British Museum — 38-59 f, 193 b) further supports this claim that Joseph of Arimathea was uncle to the Blessed Mary. It also adds he had a daughter, Anna, calling her "consobrina" or cousin of Mary.

Other early historical manuscripts refer to Joseph as "Joseph de Marmore" or Arimathea. "Mar," is an Eastern term for lord and "more" or "mawe" signifies "great." Thus the title would mean, "the Great Lord Joseph of Arimathea," a title in keeping with his birth as a prince of the House of David.

It is quite obvious that the husband (Joseph the widower and carpenter) of Mary died while Jesus was young. Under both Roman and Hebrew law, the next male kin automatically becomes the legal guardian of the family. In this case it was Joseph of Arimathea. Had there been blood brothers this duty would have passed to the eldest. The children of Mary's husband, Joseph, were by a former marriage. The term "brothers" (and sisters) in the Scriptures was only one of domestic association. We also note their mother was a sister-in-law of Zachariah, making them full cousins to John the Baptist. (Jerome's "Adiv Jovianum" libri II, compiled in Bethlehem 393 A.D.)

We also cannot overlook the fact that Joseph *"went in boldly unto*

Pilate ... and (Pilate) *gave the body to Joseph."* (Mark 15:43-45) The Sanhedrin had declared Jesus a criminal. According to both Roman and Jewish law, unless the body of an executed criminal was immediately claimed by the next of kin, the body of the victim was cast into a common pit, where as with others, all physical record of them was completely obliterated. Certainly, the fanatical Sadducean element of the Sanhedrin who sought the total extinction of Jesus, even in death, would have allowed nothing short of a legal claim on the body of Christ.

Joseph of Arimathea was a man whom the Sadducees dared not oppose. His influence was so great it stretched beyond the borders of Judea into the high places of Roman authority. The hatred of the Sadducees toward Joseph must have been surpassed only by their hatred of Jesus. It was Joseph who, on at least one occasion, defended Jesus before the Sanhedrin. Throughout the trial Jesus offered no defense, knowing beforehand He was destined to die.

There is reason to believe that Joseph of Arimathea was not present at the final trial of Jesus before the Sanhedrin. Being aware of the mystery of the birth of Jesus, Joseph must have been aware of His destiny. Joseph believed in the validity of all Jesus taught and ultimately suffered for. (Gospel of Nicademus 9:5-11) It is also possible that Christ Himself asked Joseph not to appear in His defense. Joseph's presence might have delayed the inevitable appointment with the Cross.

Although Matthew and Mark declared that *"all the chief priests and elders"* and the *"whole council"* was present at the morning trial, it is possible they were employing a figure of speech, (synedoche — a figure of speech in which a part or individual is used for a whole or class, or the reverse of this) when they said that *"all the council"* was present.

A number of arguments have been offered to indicate that more than one of the members of the Sanhedrin were absent at the morning trial of Jesus. (There were two distinct trials: one between 2 and 3 AM Friday, which is recorded by Matthew 5 and Mark 6, and a second about daybreak of the same day, recorded by Matthew 7, Mark 8 and Luke 9). In the first place, at a previous meeting of the Sanhedrin, it has been said, Nicodemus, a Pharisee by profession, and a member of the Sanhedrin, defended Jesus by asking his fellow-judges this question: "Doth our law judge any man before it hear him and know what he doeth? " There is no good reason to believe that Nicodemus defended Jesus at this meeting and then turned against Him at a subsequent one. This would also be true of Joseph of Arimathea who "had not consented to the council and deed of them."

The trial of Jesus was held in illegal session and in breach of Roman law as well as Hebrew law. The Roman law did not permit court hearings to be held after sunset. The Hebrew law forbid a trial for life since this was the exclusive perogative of the Roman Courts, and held only before the Roman Procurator. Yet, Caiaphas, High Priest of the Sanhedrin, ordered and presided over the trial of Jesus in which the death penalty was demanded.

Recognizing that only Roman authority could impose a death sentence, Caiaphas demanded that Jesus be tried before Pontius Pilate, the Roman Procurator of the Roman Province of Palestine, on the charge of treason. It is quite possible Joseph pleaded with Pilate on Jesus' behalf. Four times Pilate pronounced Jesus innocent of all charges. Yet, in the tangle of politics and intrigue, Jesus was condemned and executed as a common criminal. His body was placed in the tomb which Joseph had provided for himself, within the confines of his garden (orchard) at Jerusalem. Joseph continued to hold his membership in the Sanhedrin until the year 36 A.D.

GARDEN TOMB-JERUSALEM

Strangely, the Bible has nothing further to say about Joseph of Arimathea, following the Crucifixion. Surely this man who was a disciple of Jesus; who had shown rare courage in begging the body of Jesus, would have become a close follower of Christ after the transforming experience at Pentecost. The Bible never mentions him again, yet we are not left in the dark concerning the dominant role Joseph played in the spreading of Christianity. Joseph became the Apostle of Britain, who with twelve other disciples of Christ, including his son, Josephes, and Mary the mother of Jesus, established Christianity in the Isles of Britain over five hundred years before St. Augustine set foot on English soil.

Several ancient manuscripts indicate that after the Passion of Christ, Joseph of Arimathea was commissioned by St. Philip, the Apostle, to take the Gospel to Britain. One such manuscript is the "Victory of Aurelius Ambrosius" by Gildas Albanicus. It asserts plainly that Britain received the Gospel in the time of Emperor Tiberius, and that Joseph was sent, with others (after the dispersion of the Disciples) to Britain by St. Philip. There, Joseph was to lay the foundation of the Christian religion. The author gives the date "about the year of Our Lord 63" and adds that Joseph stayed in Britain the rest of his life.

Another manuscript, "De Antiquities of Glastonbury" (1908), contains this entry in the opening chapter: "St. Philip ... coming into the country of the Franks to preach ... converted to the Faith, and baptized them. Working to spread Christ's word, he chose twelve from among his disciples, and sent them into Britain. Their leader, it was said, was Philip's dearest friend, Joseph of Arimathea, who buried the Lord." (Translated from "De Antiquite Glastonbiensis Ecclesia" 1240)

Hugh Paulinus Cressy, the English Catholic Benedictine (1605-1674), in his "Church History of England" describes Britain as receiving the "beams of the Sun of Righteousness before many other countries nearer approaching the place where He first rose." (Book 1, Chapter 5) "Now the most eminent of the primitive disciples, and who contributed most to this heavenly building, was St. Joseph of Arimathea, and eleven of his companions with him, among whom is reckoned his son of his own name. These toward the latter end of Nero's reign, and before St. Peter and St. Paul were consummated by a glorious martyrdom, are by the testimony of ancient records said to have entered this island, as a place for the retiredness of it, the benignity to the British Princes, and the freedom from Roman tyranny, more, opportune, and better prepared for entertaining the Gospel of Peace, than almost any country, under the Romans." (Book 2, Chapter 1)

Gildas Badonicus, (A.D. 516 - 570) the earliest British historian, refers to Joseph of Arimathea as "nobilis decurio." The same title, "Decurio" is used by St. Jerome in his translation of the Vulgate of St. Mark's "honourable counsellor" (Mark 15:43) and St. Luke's "counsellor." (Luke 23:50) In the Roman world, a "decurio" denoted an important Roman office, usually connected with the general management of a mining district. The implication is that Joseph was a provincial (Britain?) Roman Senator and in charge of Rome's mining interests in Britain. Such a position would require Joseph to spend a considerable amount of time away from his homeland. This would also account for the reason the Evangelists had so little to say about him. He was busy in the metal trade in Britain.

THE METAL TRADE OF BRITAIN

We have abundant evidence that a flourishing metal trade existed in Britain long before the Christian era. As early as 1500 B.C., Phoenician and Hebrew merchants plied their ships in the coastal waters of the British Isles to barter for tin and other metals of the islands. The Greek historian, Herodotus, writing in the 5th century B.C. makes reference to the metal trade with the "Isles of the West," calling them the "Cassiterides" or "Tin Islands" — Cassiterite being an ore of tin.

Diodorus Siculus (the Roman historian) writing in the first century B.C., also describes the metal trade and writes of how the Phoenician ships, "voyaged beyond the Pillars of Heracles into the sea that men call the ocean." During the 7th and 6th centuries B.C. the Phoenicians sailed the "Hippos," a long range, deep sea-going craft that could remain at sea for a year or more. Archaeological evidence of these Phoenician ships are found on wall reliefs excavated from the palace of Sargon II, in Assyria.

RELIEF FROM PALACE OF SARGON II
SHOWING PHOENICIAN SHIPS TOWING LOGS OF CEDARWOOD

Pytheas (353 - 323 B.C.) wrote about the tin trade with Britain, as did Polybeus. (160 B.C.) Diodorus describes the ancient tin industry of mining and smelting as follows: "They that inhabit the British promontory of Belerium, by reason of their converse with the merchants, are more civilized and courteous to strangers than the rest. These are the people that make the tin, which with a great deal of care and labour they dig out of the ground; and that being rocky, the metal is mixed with some veins of earth, out of which they melt the metal and then refine it. Then they beat it into four square pieces like a die and carry it to a British isle, near at hand, called Ictis. For at low tide, all being dry between them and the island, they convey over in carts abundance of tin." (Book V, cap. 2)

ST. MICHAEL'S MOUNT

This description of the island as being joined to the mainland at low tide, describes St. Michael's Mount, a small island off the southern coast of Cornwall, in southern England. The Mount is dedicated to St. Michael, the Archangel, who is said to have appeared to a group of fishermen (in 495 A.D.) on a ledge high above the waves on the western side of the island. The visitation of the Archangel made the Mount a place of pilgrimage. Its recognition as a religious center came in 1044 A.D., when Edward the Confessor established a cell there and granted its administration to the Abbot of Mount St. Michael. By the fourteenth century, a castle and a church were built on the island. Today, a cluster of cottages front the miniature harbor of the island. At low tide, a causeway links the island to the village of Marazion, on the mainland of Cornwall.

In the little harbor of the island, in 1969, a stone bowl was found by skin-divers and placed in the island museum. This author, visiting the island a few weeks later, identified the bowl as "Phoenician" and dating about 1500 B.C. Subsequently, the identification and date was confirmed by representatives of the British Museum. Such a bowl could have been used to measure tin, which in those early days would have been like grains of metal washed out of the sands and gravels along the banks of the Cornish rivers.

PHOENICIAN STONE BOWL DATED ABOUT 1500 B.C.

The tin mines of Cornwall were the source of the world's supply of tin (the chief metal for making alloys) in the first century A.D. The remains of mining in the county are widespread and found in almost every parish except in north Cornwall. From the muddy waters of the Tamar River which forms the county's eastern boundary, to the very edge of the cliffs, by Land's End, ore has been extracted from the ground. Gaunt granite engine-houses, crumbling brick stack, water-wheel pits, old count-houses, innumerable shafts and pits, and over-grown adit portals, remind us that this is a mineralized area which has been more intensively mined than any other in Britain — in fact than in most of Europe.

Geologists explain the reasons for the occurrance of tin, as well as other metals, such as lead, copper and zinc, in Cornwall and Devon. The different minerals lie in roughly concentric zones, with the inner-

AN ENGRAVING OF LEVANT MINE ON THE CLIFFS AT ST. JUST (1847)

most one encircling an "emanative center." Roughly speaking, this is a point where mineral-bearing liquids or vapors rose from the molten granite. In this innermost zone the higher temperature mineral, tin, crystallized out first. Around it, where temperatures were lower, lies the copper zone, and around that, in turn, is a much wider band containing the lower temperature minerals. These comprise zinc blende, lead ore, silver and iron ores.

Although it is certain that the production of tin in Cornwall (and Devon) is an industry of great antiquity, true vein (lode) mining, as a major method of production, did not commence until the Middle Ages. Most of the tin in the early days was obtained by "streaming," that is, by washing it out from alluvial deposits along side streams and in valley bottoms. The grains of tin would sometimes be melted into ingots for ease of shipping. Many such Pre-Roman relics have been found. One, known as the "St. Mawes Tin Ingot," was found in the Fal Estuary in 1812. It weighs over 158 pounds and can be seen today in the Truto Museum, in Cornwall.

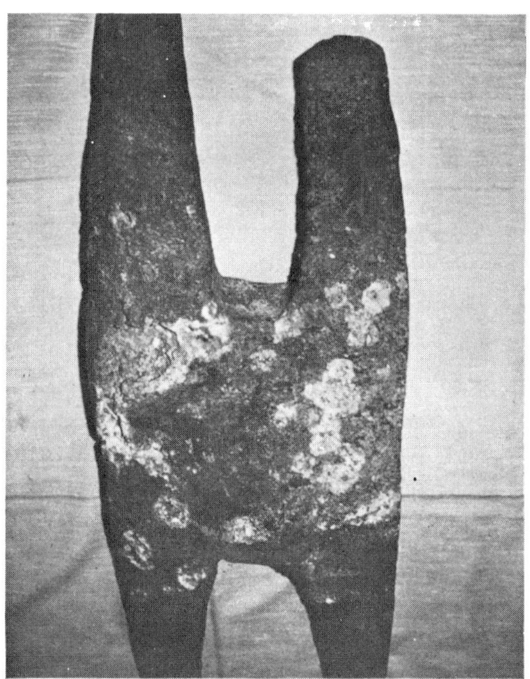

ST. MAWES TIN INGOT

The first attempts at true mining (exploiting an actual lode) were almost certainly made in the coastal regions of western Cornwall, near St. Just. Here, lodes exposed in the cliffs could be attacked by the level (or gallery) driven in from there. The same technique could be applied wherever there was a lode out cropping in a valley, or on a hillside. It was in such favored localities that the first actual mines began in Cornwall.

The Glastonbury Tradition that Joseph was actually engaged in the tin trade is only tradition, however, it is fairly ancient and widespread. Fragments of poems and miner's songs, handed down through the centuries, make frequent reference to Joseph. One refrain runs, "Joseph was a tin man, Joseph was in the tin trade." (Cornwall, S. Baring-Gould, Pg. 57) There is scarcely a spot in Cornwall where tin has been mined that does not have some Hebrew names still adhering to the site. Since earliest times, the old smelting places of Cornwall have been referred to as "Jew's Houses, (Polwhele's History of Cornwall - 1803) meaning of course, "Judahites" — from the Israelite tribe of Judah, to which Joseph of Arimathea belonged.

Historical evidence exists that the tribe of Asher was also associated with the mining of tin in Cornwall. Camden, in his first volume of Britannica, published in 1808, states clearly: "The merchants of Asher worked the tin mines of Cornwall, not as slaves, but as masters and exporters." Sir Edward Shepherd Creasy, the eminent British historian (1812-1878), in his "History of England," writes; "The British mines mainly supplied the glorious adornment of Solomon's Temple."

For many years the Phoenicians of Cadiz (largely Semites — Israelite tribe of Dan) held a monopoly on the source of the British tin they transported. They guarded their secret jealously. When followed by other seacraft, hoping to learn the source of their trade, their mariners would deliberately sail a false course and in extremity would purposely wreck their vessel. This sacrifice was reinbursed out of the Phoenician treasure. Confirmation of this is found in the writings of Strabo, who died A.D. 25: "Anciently the Phoenicians alone, from Cadiz, engrossed this market, hiding the navigation from all others. When the Romans followed the course of a vessel that they might discover the situation, the jealous pilot willfully stranded the ship, misleading those who were tracing him to the same destruction. Escaping from the shipwreck, he was indemnified for his losses out of the public treasury." The Phoenicians of Cadis kept the secret of the tin mines so well, it wasn't until 450 B.C. that the elusive Tin Islands were discovered by Hamilco, a Phoenician of Carthage, who sailed through the Straits of Gilbralter, and in going north discovered Cornwall, England.

Several legends link Joseph of Arimathea and the boy Jesus with the tin mines of Cornwall. One story relates how Jesus, visiting the mines with his uncle Joseph, taught the miners how to extract tin and purge it of the ore wolframite. Another story tells how Jesus and

Joseph often anchored their ship in the natural harbor at the mouth of the Camel River to come ashore and collect water for the ship. Nearby, is an ancient well that since olden times has been known as "Jesus' Well." It was regarded as having healing powers. For centuries pilgrims came to the well and the remains of a chapel, erected over it, are still discernible. Records of its existence go back to the 13th century, but even then, the date and origin of its name is unknown.

JESUS WELL NEAR PADSTOW — CORNWALL

Another Cornish link between Jesus and the tin trade of Britain is found in the almost unknown "Place Manor Church" of St. Anthony-in-Roseland. In the Pre-Norman stone arch over the South Door of the Church is carved a story in ancient pictographs. The carvings are over 1000 years old and display an anchor, a Lamb and Cross insignia, a symbol of Jesus Christ, the Lamb of God. The story told by the carvings is of Jesus and His uncle coming to Place for tin. Their boat got into difficulties, during a storm, and washed ashore on the headland where the modern lighthouse now stands. The local inhabitants (operating the trading post there) brought Joseph's damaged boat into the lee of the headland by Place. While repairs were being made, Joseph and Jesus stayed there, and before they left they erected a little shrine with an account of their visit there.

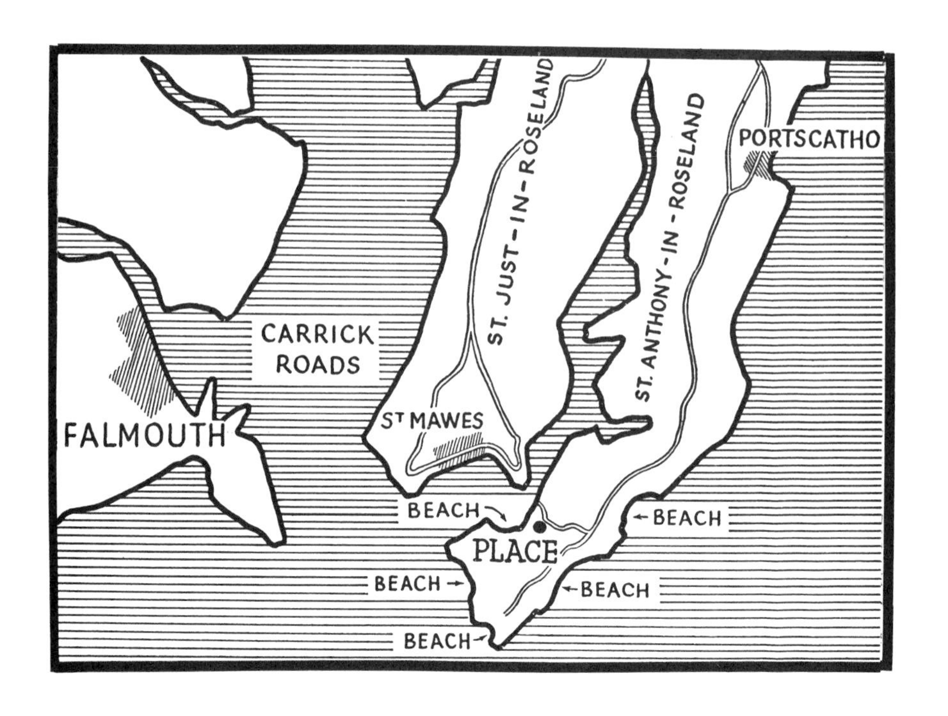

PLACE MANOR - FROM AN OLD PRINT

The pictographs (carvings) were interpreted by an archaeologist familiar with Egyptian and Phoenician symbols. He stated that he had seen similar symbols on a doorway to one of the temples at Denderah, in Lower Egypt, belonging to the later Hyksos Dynasties. His interpretation not only confirmed the coming of Jesus to Place, but His birth and the date of His suffering. Part of the interpretation is "The Lamb and the Cross are facing the rising sun — this means that He was here in the early years of life. His future was before Him. Because He is on the left of the center line — it means He was here in December." (The Story of Place - by Edward Harte)

SOUTH DOOR ARCH OF PLACE MANOR

Since the Hyksos Dynasties were Hebrew Phoenicians in origin, there is no mystery as to the use of Phoenician symbols in Cornwall. Logically, we may suppose that after thousands of years contact with the Phoenician traders, the Cornish people would have been greatly influenced by their civilization. This influence extended even to the early Celts worshipping the same gods. Thus, the Celtric Priesthood was initiated into their rituals — learning and using the symbolical (esoteric) signs of the Phoenicians. This knowledge continued on down the ages and into the early Christian times. Just as the Phoenicians used Ogham script (an early form of linear writing) so did the early Celts.

Ogham writing has only 16 characters, but it has inumerable permutations (changes in arrangement of position) similar to shorthand. The same symbol on the front of a stone has a different meaning when inscribed on the left side. This is a very early method of writing Ogham where a rough line is drawn down the center of the face of a stone, with the characters inscribed on each side. Many examples of Ogham writing are found in Ireland.

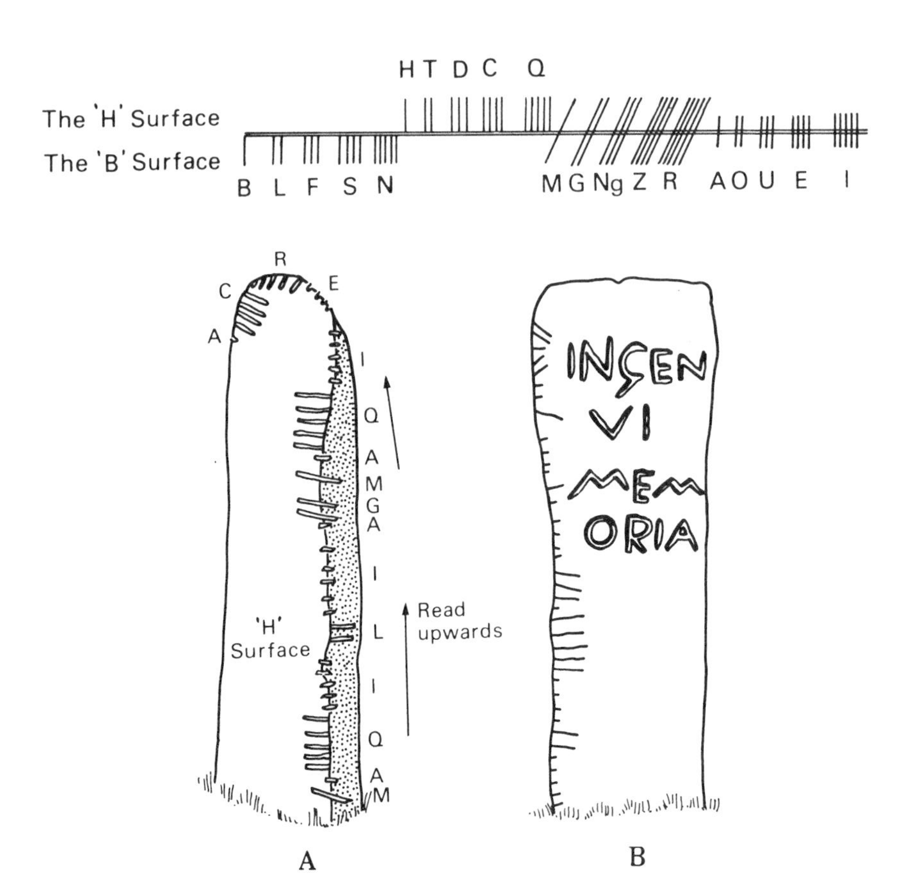

The Ogham alphabet - short and long strokes, above, below, across and through the line. (A) Tombstone of MAQILIAG son of ERCA from county Kerry, Ireland (B) Sixth-century bilingual tombstone from Cornwall; the Ogham reads INGENAVIMEMOR.

An example of Ogham script is found on a panel in the Spry Memorial Chapel (in the North Transept) of the Place Manor Church. Experts in ancient writing are in agreement that the writing is not later than the end of the first century A.D. or at the latest, the beginning of the second. The panel tells the same story as the carvings over the South Door of the Church. The inscription starts with the ancient sign of "Icthus," the fish. To the early Christians, "Icthus" stood for "Jesus Christ-God-Son-Saviour," the first letter of each word spelling "Ichtus" which is the Greek word for fish. Below the fish is found the top portion of a ship with its sails furled, meaning the ship was at anchor. Next, we see Our Lord's Head with the Crown of Thorns, meaning the inscription was carved after He was Crucified. If it is true that Jesus once stayed here this would mean the inscription had been carved as a memorial to that event.

The lighthouse at Place was built in 1835 on the foundation of an ancient chapel dedicated to St. Ann (our Lord's grandmother) who came from just across the channel, in Brittany. In ancient times, they often built small chapels to commemorate events. It seems significant that all through the 1500 years that monks lived at St. Anthony Monastery one of their principle duties was to keep a light burning on those rocks to warn ships away. This was long before lighthouses were ever thought of on the Cornish coast.

St. Just, in Cornwall, also has legends of Jesus coming to Cornwall. Among the many traditions is one that tells of a stone that Jesus stepped on when he first landed here. In 1932, a flat stone was found by workmen cleaning out a culvert that had become blocked by debris. This stopped the flow of water from a well known as the "Christening Well," a name whose origin is lost in antiquity. The stone was covered with curious and unintelligible markings. The question comes to mind — could this be the stone of the legend? Perhaps marked at some later date when the identity of their visitor became known? The inhabitants of the district think so. Even before the finding of the stone, the old folks would tell visitors to the area, the Holy Legend of Christ coming there as a young boy with His uncle. They spoke of the legend and "it was as much as your life was worth" to express any doubt about Christ coming to St. Just.

In the west part of Cornwall were two rich lodes or veins of tin, recorded on the old Ordinance maps, having the names, "Corpus Christi" (Body of Christ) and "Wheel of Jesus." (Wheel is an old Cornish word for 'mine') In this tin mining area of Cornwall are found a number of very ancient Celtic crosses, called "Tunic Crosses." They are found by roadsides and church yards and are of a type found nowhere else in the British Isles. On one side of the cross is a crudely cut Christian cross and on the other, the figure of what can only be a boy, dressed in a knee-length tunic. Here we have not a crucified Christ, nailed to a cross, but a youth with his arms outstretched in an attitude of blessing. These crosses may well portray the age-old memory of the visits of the young Jesus to these shores in the company of His uncle Joseph.

TUNIC CROSSES

Associated with the mines of Cornwall are the mines of the Mendip Hills, north of Glastonbury, in the county of Somerset, England. These mines produced lead, copper and other metals which form alloys with tin. Traditions among the hill folk of Somerset relate that Joseph, after first seeking tin from the Scillies (islands) and Cornwall, came to the Mendips and was accompanied on several occasions by the boy Jesus. At the parish Church of Priddy, high on top of the Mendips, they have an old saying: "As sure as our Lord was at Priddy." And a carol sung by the children of Priddy begins: "Joseph was a tin merchant, a tin merchant, a tin merchant," and goes on to describe him arriving from the sea in a boat.

Two "pigs" (bars) of lead were found near the mines of the Mendips. One was dated A.D. 49 and has the name of "Britannicus," son of the Emperor Claudius, stamped upon it. This indicates that the mining of lead was being pursued there in the time of Christ. The other bar of lead was dated A.D. 60 and bore the inscription "British lead, the property of the Emperor Nero." In 1956, four bars of lead were found at a farm near the village of Pilton. These bore the name of Emperor Vespasian of the Roman occupation of Britain (A.D. 69-79). This was the very same Vespasian who, with his son, fulfilled Christ's prophecy concerning the destruction of Jerusalem in A.D. 70.

PIGS (INGOTS) OF LEAD

Specimens of Roman-British lead (from the Mendip mines) have been found in various parts of the Roman Empire. About 1950 an ancient Roman drain-pipe, bonded with lead, was found at Ostia, the sea-port of Rome. Analysis showed the lead had been mined in the Mendips. It is also said that the ancient aqueduct in Jerusalem attributed to King Solomon, used the particular type of lead found in the Mendip area. This would indicate the mining of lead in Britain before 1000 B.C.

References to the metal of Britain is also found in the writings of Pytheas (353 B.C.), Aristolle (350 B.C.), Polybius (150 B.C.) Posidonius (75 B.C.), and others, most of whom wrote long before the Christian era. So, based upon the sure foundation of a well established metal trade between Britain and the Roman world, we have the evidence for the centuries-old traditions and legends, deeply rooted in Somerset and Cornwall counties — known as the "Traditions of Glastonbury."

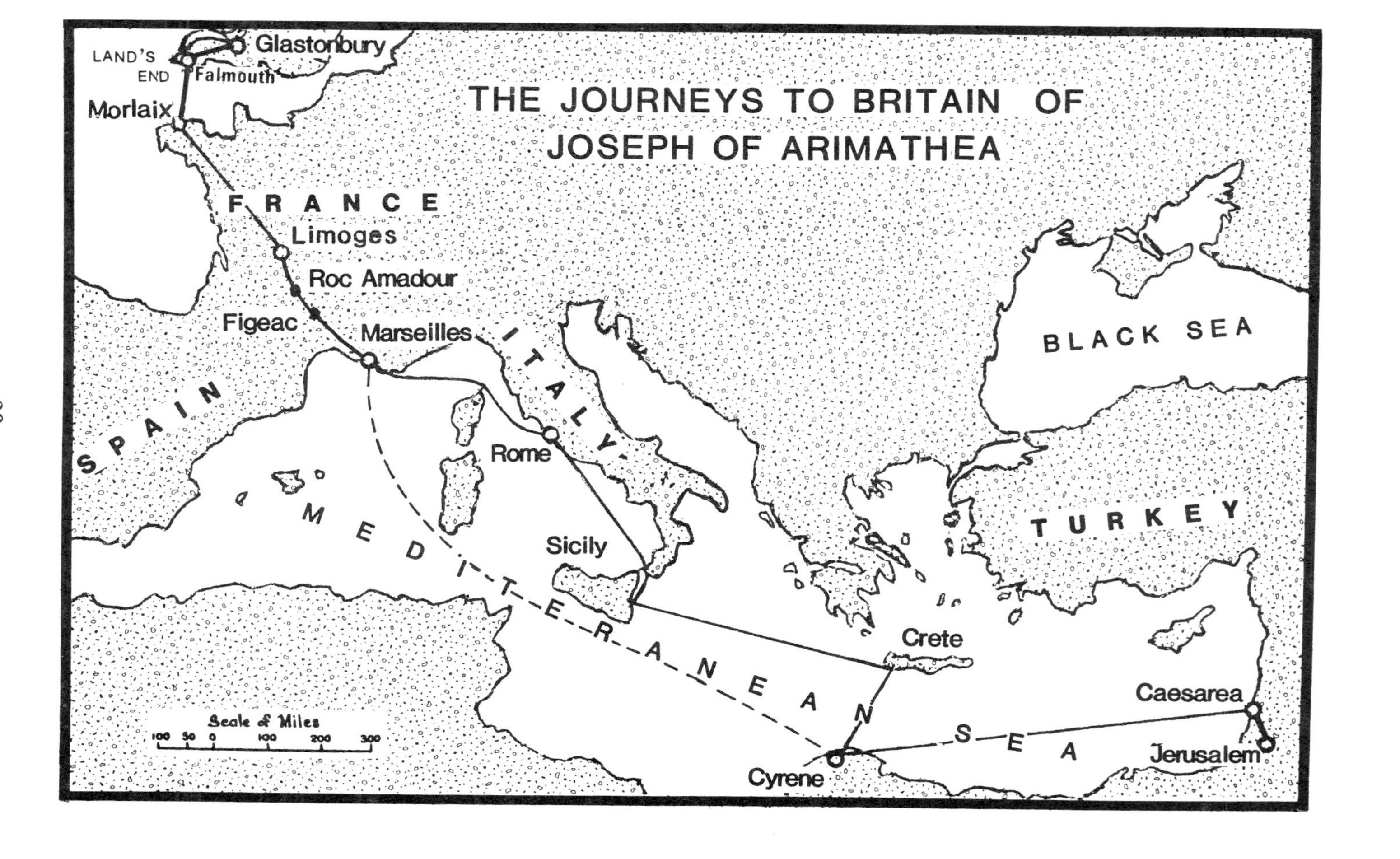
THE JOURNEYS TO BRITAIN OF
JOSEPH OF ARIMATHEA
Glastonbury
LAND'S END
Falmouth
Morlaix
FRANCE
Limoges
Roc Amadour
Figeac
Marseilles
ITALY
SPAIN
Rome
BLACK SEA
TURKEY
Sicily
MEDITERRANEAN SEA
Crete
Caesarea
Jerusalem
Cyrene
Scale of Miles
100 50 0 100 200 300

Soon after the Ascension of Christ, a great persecution of Christ's followers broke out in Jerusalem. The Bible records the death of the Church's first martyr, Stephen: *"And they stoned Stephen, calling upon God, and saying, Lord Jesus, receive my spirit,"* (Acts 7:59) and then tells us: *"And at that time there was a great persecution against the church which was at Jerusalem; and they were all scattered abroad throughout the regions of Judaea and Samaria, except the apostles. And devout men carried Stephen to his burial, and made great lamentation over him. As for Saul, he made havock of the church, entering into every house, and haling men and women committed them to prison."* (Acts 8:1-3)

James was then beheaded and Peter put into prison. (Acts 12:2-4) According to tradition, Joseph of Arimathea, with other disciples of Christ, including Mary, the mother of Jesus, were cast adrift off the coast of Caesarea by the Jewish Sanhedrin. Without sails or oars, they drifted with the wind and the currents arriving unharmed at Cyrene, in northern Africa. After obtaining sails and oars, the little party of refugees followed the trade route of the Phoenician merchant ships as far west as Marseilles, France.

Cardinal Caesar Baronius, (A.D. 1538-1609) was a learned historian and librarian to the Vatican. In his "Ecclesiastical Annals," - ending A.D. 1198 (on which he spent 30 years) identifies those that accompanied Joseph as (under section A.D. 35) "the two Bethany sisters, Mary and Martha — their brother Lazarus — St. Eutropius — St. Salome — St. Cleon — St. Saturninus — St. Mary Magdalene — Marcella (the maid of the Bethany sisters) — St. Maxim (or Maximin) — St. Martial — St. Trophimus (Restitutus, the man who was born blind). Mary the mother of Jesus undoubtedly was not left behind.

The Cardinal's Annals quote the "Acts of Magdalen" for the record of the voyage to Marseilles and the preaching of the Gospel in the south of France by the Bethany family. The original manuscript was compiled by Rabanus Maurus, Archbishop of Mayence (A.D. 766-856) and a copy is in the Magdalen College Library at Oxford, England. Chapter 37, after listing names of those accompaning Joseph, describes their voyaging: "Leaving the shores of Asia and favoured by an east wind, they went round about, down the Tyrrhenian Sea, between Europe and Africa, leaving the city of Rome and all the land of Italy to the right. Then happily turning their course to the right, they came near to the city of Marseilles, in the Viennoise province of the Gauls, where the river Rhone is received by the sea. There, having called upon God, the great King of all the world, they parted; each company going to the province where the Holy Spirit had directed them; presently preaching everywhere, 'the Lord working with them, and confirming the word with signs following'."

There are several other manuscripts, some older, some more recent than that of Rabanus (MS. Laud 108 of the Bodleian) and they all agree on the essential facts. Lazarus is reported as having become the first Bishop of Marseilles, while the names of some of the other saints are perpetuated in the records of the early Gallic Church. Roger of Hovedon (A.D. 1174-1201) the English chronicler, writing of Marseilles, says: Marseilles is an Episcopal city under the dominion of the King of Aragon. Here are the relics of St. Lazarus, ... who held the Bishopric here for seven years after Jesus had restored him from the dead." (Vol. 3. p. 51) There is no doubt that for over a thousand years the Roman Church accepted the presence of these saints in France.

While some of the party of refugees settled in France, Joseph, later, with Mary and eleven other companions crossed France to the Atlantic coast. They followed well-known Phoenician trade routes to Britain as described (before the birth of Jesus) by Diodorus Siculus. This would have taken them through the country of the Lemovices to the sea-coast in Brittany at Vannes or Morlaix. From Morlaix, according to one legend, the refugees sailed to Falmouth, England, before continuing on to Cornwall.

Two traditional routes are found in the legends of Glastonbury tracing Joseph and his disciples to their destination. One story has the little party traveling overland from Cornwall to Glastonbury. According to the other legend, the refugees sailed around the southern tip of England, passing what is today known as "Land's End." Then,

following the west coast, they sailed northward to the Severn Sea. From there they entered the estuaries of the rivers Parrot and Brue. Following the River Brue eastward, they arrived at a little cluster of islands about twelve miles inland from the coast, Joseph's destination was the Isle of Avalon, suitable as a quiet retreat in which to establish a home for Mary — a place they knew had already been hallowed by the presence of their Master.

Joseph and his companions were met by King Arviragus of the Silurian dynasty of Britain. He was the son of King Cunobelinus (the Cymbeline of Shakespeare) and cousin to the renounded British warrior, Caradoc, whom the Romans renamed "Caractacus." Undoubtedly, Arviragus and Joseph were well known to each other; Joseph's business as a metal merchant for the Romans would have brought him in contact with the King on more than one occasion. Later, King Arviragus was to play an important role in the struggle against Roman dominance of Britain.

Hardynge's Chronicle, a fifteenth-century writing based upon much earlier works, gives the following passage concerning Joseph and the first-century king, Arviragus:

"Joseph converted this King Arviragus
By his prechying to know ye laws divine
And baptisted him as write hath Nennius
The chronicler in Britain tonque full fyne
And to Christian laws made him inclyne
And gave him then a shield of sylver white
A crosse and long end overthwart full perfete
These armes were used through all Britain
For a common syne, each man to know his nacion
And thus his armes by Joseph's Creacion
Full longafore St. George was generate
Were worhipt here of mykell elder date."

From the above it seems that the Cross was recognized as a British emblem from the earliest times. Arviragus was to carry the banner of the Cross through the most bitterly fought battles between the Britons and the Romans. It is possible that this reverence for the Cross, as the most potent of symbols, made a profound impression on the mind of Constantine the Great, while he was in Britain. Having seen the Cross, would give credibility to the story of Constantine's dream (given as a vision by some writers) of a Flaming Cross with the legend, "By this conquer." In any event, Eusebius wrote that Constantine's declared intention was "to plant the Cross of Christ on the throne of the Caesars." (Ecclesiastical History) This he succeeded in doing, though many a struggle was to continue during successive reigns. Constan-

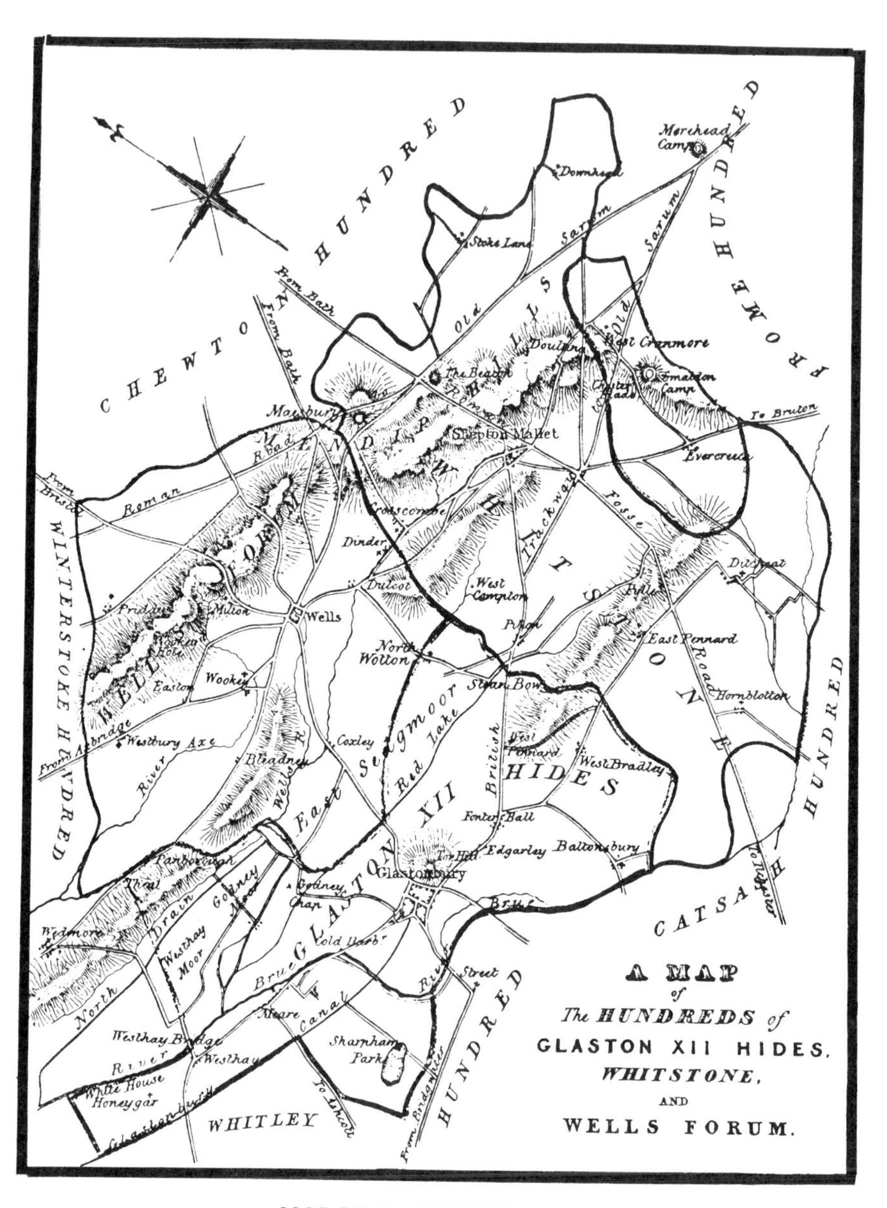

MAP OF GLASTON XII HIDES

tine's acceptance of Christianity is revealed in his "Edict of Toleration" (Milan - A.D. 313) which included a decree for the observance of both the Sabbath and Sunday. (Both days were observed by the early Christian Church). The Edict also called for the emancipation of slaves, prohibition of gladiatorial combats and crucifixion as a means of capital punishment.

King Arviragus is recorded as having granted to Joseph and his followers, "twelve hides" of land, (about 1900 acres) tax free, in "Ynis-witrin," described as a marshy tract — afterwards called the "Isle of Avalon." Confirmation of this Royal Charter is found in the official Domesday Book of Britain (A.D. 1086 which states: "The Domus Dei, in the great monastery of Glastonbury, called the Secret of the Lord. This Glastonbury Church possesses, in its own villa XII hides of land which have never paid tax." (Domesday Survey folio p. 249 b.) This notable act of the King gave the recipients many British concessions, including the right of citizenship with its privileges of freedom to pass unmolested from one district to another in time of war. The grant was given to them as "Judean refugees." (Quidam advanae-'certain strangers' —old Latin— in Later Latin, "Culdich" or Anglicised, "Culdees.")

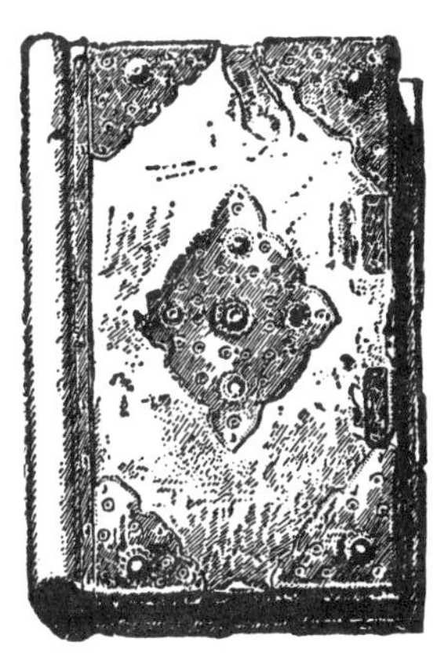

ONE VOLUME OF THE DOMESDAY BOOK

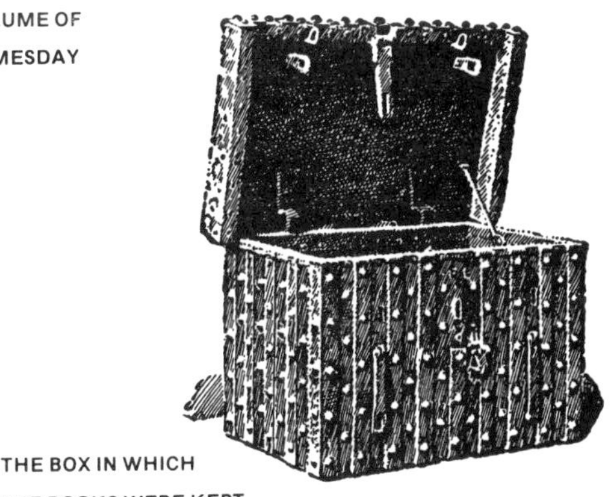

THE BOX IN WHICH THE BOOKS WERE KEPT

It should be borne in mind that the date given above, A.D. 1086, is not the date in which the Domesday Book was first written. It represents the date in which the Norman King William had all the historic events, recorded within the ancient book, rechecked and brought up to date — to his reign as King of England. The king's historian's original source of information was the Anglo-saxon Chronicle, preserved today in the British Museum. Parts of the Angle-Saxon Chronicle overlap the period of the Domesday Book; the four manuscripts ending with the following dates: A-1001, B-977, C-1066, D-1079. The later "Laud

Manuscript" ends in A.D. 1154. The Domesday Book could be a continuation of the Anglo-Saxon Chronicle.

Further confirmation of this land grant is found in the writings of William of Malmsebury, the historian of Glastonbury, a man noted for the accuracy of his works. He wrote in 1126 A.D. an account of "the writings of the ancients," which he said he found in the Glastonbury Abbey. (destroyed in 1184 A.D.) These writings included the following: "In the year of our Lord, 63, twelve holy missionaries, with Joseph of Arimathea (who had buried the Lord) at their head, came over to Britain, preaching the Incarnation of Jesus Christ. The king of the country and his subjects refused to become proselytes to their teaching, but in consideration that they had come a long journey, and being somewhat pleased with their soberness of life and unexceptional behaviour, the king, at their petition, gave them for their habitation a certain island bordering on his region, covered with trees and bramble bushes and surrounded by marshes, called Ynis-wytrin."

Having gained legal title to the land from King Arviragus, Joseph and his companions proceeded to build huts for themselves and for Mary who accompanied Joseph to Britain. They then erected what must have been the first Christian Church above ground. These early hutments would have been made from wattle daubed with mud and built in a circular form. From studies made by the late F. Bligh Bond, F.R.I.B.A. (member of the Somerset Archaeological Society and formerly director of excavations at Glastonbury Abbey) the first church was circular, having a diameter of 25 feet, with the twelve huts of the other disciples forming a circle around it. All the buildings were enclosed in a circular stockade to keep out wild animals. It was the center building that may have incorporated or covered the earlier structure built by the hands of Christ Himself.

The Abbey records, quoted by William Malmsebury, continues with an interesting statement: "These holy men built a chapel of the form that had been shown them. The walls were of osiers wattled together." Although Malmsebury describes the wattle church as "rude and misshapen," its wall were undoubtedly built in the mode of the day — timbered pillars and framework, doubly wattled inside and out, its roof thatched with reeds. Often painted or washed with lime, these wattle buildings withstood the most severe weather. Even castles, in those days, were built of the same material. Giraldus Cambrensis, speaking of Pembroke Castle wrote: "Arnulphus de Montgomery, in the days of Henry I (A.D. 1068-1135) built a small castle of twigs and slight turf." The primitive Capital of Rome (Ovid 'Faesti ad Fest Roma') was of similar construction.

The words, describing the chapel as in the "form that had been shown them" are intriguing. Did they find the earlier home of Mary and the boy Jesus, probably in ruins? And, was it used as a model or itself rebuilt into a home for Mary? And after her death, was it used as a Chapel?

ST. AUGUSTINE

Testimony to such an early 'church' is found in a letter of Augustine to Pope Gregory (A.D. 600) which reads: "In the western confines of Britain, there is a certain royal island of large extent, surrounded by water, abounding in all the beauties of nature and necessities of life. In it, the first neophites of Catholic law, God beforehand acquainting them, found a church constructed by no human art, but by the hands of Christ Himself, for the salvation of His people." (Epistolae ad Gregorium Papam)

We cannot tell whether Augustine's words "constructed by no human art" referred to a building erected by Jesus or to the fact that the Glastonbury Christian community was established on a 'foundation' laid by Christ Himself. However, the original wattle building would have been over 500 years old, if existing, a remarkable age for a structure of such material.

THE FIRST CHRISTIAN CHURCH IN BRITAIN

The admission of this early origin of the British Church by a Roman Church official (who had been rebuffed by the same church) is remarkable testimony. It was to St. Augustine that the British Bishop (and Abbot of Bangor) Diaothus replied to the question of deferring to Rome: "Be it known and declared that we all, individually and collectively, are in all humility prepared to defer to the Church of God, and to the Bishop of Rome, and to every sincere and godly Christian, so far as to love every one according to his degree, in perfect charity, and to assist them all by word and in deed in becoming the children of God. But as for any other obedience, we know of none that he whom you term Pope, or Bishop of Bishops, can demand. The deference we have mentioned we are ready to pay to him as to every other Christian, but in all other respects our obedience is due to the jurisdiction of the Bishop of Caerlon, who is alone under God our ruler to keep us right in the way of salvation." (Spelman's Concilia, pp. 108, 109; Haddan and Stubbs, Vol. 1, pg. 122)

Bede, the English historian and theologian (672-735) in his "Ecclesiastical History of the English Nation" gives this account of the faith of the British Church at the coming of Augustine: "For they did not keep Easter Sunday at the proper time, but from the fourteenth to the twentieth moon; which computation is contained in a revolution of eighty-four years. Besides, they did several other things which were against the unity of the Church ... After a long disputation, they did not comply with the entreaties, exhortations, or rebukes of Augustine and his companions, but preferred their own traditions before all the churches in the world ... They could not depart from their ancient customs without the consent of their people." (J.M. Dent, Everyman's Edn., pp. 65-66)

We read of the Wattle Church, called by the Angles, the "Ealde Churche" or "Old Church" being encased in boards and covered with lead by St. Paulinus, (A.D. 625-644) the Archbishop of York and, afterwards, the Bishop of Rochester. Later, a stone church was erected over it; the old church thus being preserved intact, inside. The Wattle Church became known as the "Culdee Church" or "Church of the Refugees."

In the ancient British Triads, Joseph and his twelve companions are refered to as "Culdees" as were Paul, Peter, Lazarus, Simon Zelotes, Aristobulus and others. As this name was not known outside of Britain, it therefore could only have been assigned to those who had actually dwelt in Celtric Britain. In later years, the name "Culdee" took on added significance, emphasizing the fact that the Culdee Christian Church was the original Church of Christ on earth. It became a title applied to the early British Church for centuries, even after the name had died out elsewhere in favour of the more popular name, "Christian."

The word "Christian" is a composite of Greek and Hebrew. "Christ" is the Greek word meaning "consecrated," and "ian" is from the Hebrew word "ain" meaning a person or people. Therefore, the true meaning of the words, "Christian" and "Christians" would be a "consecrated person" and "consecrated people." It is quite likely that the term "Christian" as applied to a nation, was first used in Britain if one accepts as valid the statement by Sabellus (an early Christian presbyter and theologian) written in A.D. 250: "Christianity was privately confessed elsewhere, but the (first) nation that proclaimed it as their religion and (called it Christian) after the name of Christ, was Britain." This confirms Gildas Badonicus' statement that "Joseph introduced Christianity into Britain in the last year of the reign of Tiberius."

There is nothing more striking in the history of the early British

Church than its missionary zeal in the face of constant harassment. The constant raids of the heathen Saxons, their demolition of churches, monasteries and manuscripts took a heavy toll in both property and lives. After the Saxons were converted, similar raids by their still heathen kinsmen, the Danes, nearly wiped out the Christian Church in the Isles, except in portions of Western England.

The first converts of the Culdees or "Judean refugees" were the Druids of Britain, who found no difficulty in reconciling the teaching of the Culdees with their own teaching of the resurrection and inheritance of eternal life. Many writers have noted the remarkable coincidence which exists between the two systems — Druidism and Christianity. Before the introduction of Christianity to Britain, the Druids made reference to the Supreme God as: "Distributor," "Governor," "The Wonderful," "The Ancient of Days," terms of Old Testament origin. (Religion of Ancient Britain by G. Smith, Chap. II, pg. 37)

The overwhelming Continental influence of the Roman Church, in the 8th century A.D., reinforced by the Norman Conquest, finally caused the memory of the Culdee Church to be nearly eclipsed. Culdees are recorded in church documents as officiating at St. Peter, York, until A.D. 939. According to some church authorities, the Canons of York were called "Culdees" as late as the reign of Henry II. (A.D. 1133-1189) In Ireland, a whole county was named "Culdee." The names "Culdee" and "Culdish" clung tenaciously to the Scottish Church, and its prelates, until a much late date.

"The pure Culdees
were Alby's (Albion) earliest priests of God,
ere yet an island of her seas
by foot of Saxon monk was trod."

(Reullura by Campbell)

Support for the coming of Joseph and his companions shortly after the Resurrection is found in several sources: Tertullian (A.D. 155-222) whose full name was "Quintus Septimus Florens Terullianus" is the earliest, and after Augustine, the greatest of the ancient church writers of the West. In his "Tertullian Def. Fidei," pg. 179, he wrote: "The extremities of Spain, the various parts of Gaul, the regions of Britain which have never been penetrated by Roman arms have received the religion of Christ."

Eusebius, (A.D. 260-340) Bishop of Caesarea, and Father of Ecclesiastical History, wrote: "The Apostles passed beyond the ocean to the isles called the Britannic Isles." (De Demonstratione Evengelii, Lib III) Having taken an active part in the Council of Nicaea, (A.D. 325)

Eusebius could have based his words on information from the British bishops in attendance.

St. Hilary of Pottiers (A.D. 300-367) wrote: "Afterwards the Apostles built several tabernacles, and through all the parts of the earth wherever it was possible to go; even in the Isles of the ocean they built several habitations for God." (Tract in XIV., Psalm 8, Haddan and Stubbs, Vol. 1, pg. 5) Another historian and Christian bishop in Gaul, Arnobius the Younger (About A.D. 400) wrote: "So swiftly runs the Word of God that within the space of a few years His Word is concealed neither from the Indians in the East, nor from the Britons in the West."

Chrysostom, (A.D. 347-407), the venerable Patriarch of Constantinople, wrote in his "Sermo De Utilit": "The British Isles which are beyond the sea, and which lie in the ocean, have received virture of the Word. Churches are there found and altars erected ... Though thou shouldst go to the ocean, to the British Isles, there thou shouldst hear all men everywhere discoursing matters out of the scriptures, with another voice indeed, but not another faith, with a different tongue, but the same judgment."

Gildas Badonicus, who referred to Joseph of Arimathea as "Nobilus Decurion" wrote: "These islands, stiff with cold and frost, and in distant region of the world, remote from the visible sun received the beams of light, that is the holy precepts of Christ, at the latter part, as we know, of the reign of Tiberius Caesar."

Since Tiberius died A.D. 37, Gildas probably means that the light of the Gospel reached Britain in that year, only four years after the Resurrection. This is also the date of the persecution of the Church of Saul of Tarus, when *"they were all scattered abroad."* (Acts 8:1) Gilda's statement also strongly supports the words of another Gildas, Gildas the Wise Albanicus (A.D. 425-512) that Britain received the Gospel in the time of Emperor Tiberius.

The traditions of the coming of Joseph to Britain was well known in later centuries. Polydore Vergil, the learned Italian historian in England wrote: "Britain, partly Joseph of Arimathea, was of all kingdoms, first, that received the Gospel". This was also recognized by four Church Councils of the 15th century — those of Pisa, (1409) Constance, (1417) Sienna, (1424) and Basle, (1434) which held that: "The churches of France and Spain, must yield in point of antiquity and precedence to that of Britain, as the latter Church was founded by Joseph of Arimathea immediately after the Passion of Christ."

From the dates given and the authorities quoted above, both secular and ecclesiastical, it is evident that Christianity (Culdee Church) flourished in Britain approximately A.D. 36-39 and the first

Christian Church above ground was erected approximately A.D. 39-41. The Roman Catholic hierarchy was founded about A.D. 350, after Constantine. Not until centuries later was the Papal title created. Until then, the head of the Roman Catholic Church was still a Bishop. The title of "Pope," or universal Bishop, was first given to the Bishop of Rome by the Emperor Phocas, in the year A.D. 610. This, he did to spite Bishop Ciracus of Constantinople, who had justly excommunicated him for his having caused the assassination of his predecessor, Emperor Mauritus. Gregory I, then Bishop of Rome, refused the title. But, his successor, Boniface III, accepted and assumed the title of "Pope."

It should be noted that Jesus did not appoint Peter to the headship of the Apostles and expressly forbade any such notion, as stated in Luke 22:24-26; Ephesians 1:22-23; I Corinthians 3:11; and Colossians 1:18.

The first Christian Church above ground in Rome is dated about A.D. 56, when St. Paul dedicated the home (Palatium Britaanicus) of the British royal Princess Claudia and her husband Rufus Pudens Pudentius. Pudens, as he was most commonly called, was a Roman Senator and former personal aide to the Roman Commander-in-Chief, Aulus Plautius. Dating from the marriage of Claudia and Pudens (several years prior to the coming of Paul to Rome) their home had been the meeting place for Christian gathered to worship. Hermas (mentioned in Romans 16:14) conducted the services.

When St. Paul appeared in Rome he ordained Linus, the brother of Claudia and son of Caractacus, to be the First Bishop of the Christian church at Rome. St. Peter affirms this fact in his "The Apostolic Constitutions": Concerning those Bishops who have been ordained in our lifetime, we make known to you that they are these: Of Antioch, Eudius, ordained by me, Peter, Of the Church of Rome, Linus brother of Claudia, first ordained by Paul, and after Linus' death, Clemens, the second ordained by me, Peter. (Bk 1, ch. 46)

Confirmation of Linus becoming the First Bishop of Rome is found in two other sources: Irenaeus (Bishop of Lyons - A.D. 180) who was personally acquainted with the first Church in Rome wrote: "The Apostles having founded and built up the church at Rome, committed the ministry of its supervision to Linus. This is the Linus mentioned by Paul in his Epistles to Timothy." (Irenace Opera 3:1) The Encyclopedia Britannica names Linus as the First Bishop of Rome.

Linus is believed to have been baptized and confirmed in Britain (possibly by Joseph of Arimathea) long before being taken hostage with Caractacus to Rome. If so, then the Church at Rome had its roots in the Culdee Church of Britain.

VETUSTA ECCLESIA

The most hallowed of all the Traditions of Glastonbury is the story of Mary, the mother of Jesus, ending her last days on earth at Glastonbury. She is said to have been intered in its sacred ground, to become the first of a long list of saints buried at Glastonbury. The list (still extant) recording the names of those buried at Glastonbury is most illustrious and unique, superior to any other cemetery in the world. Since time immemorial, the old cemetery, along side the Mary's Chapel, has been called "the most holiest ground in earth;" "the most hallowed spot in Christendom;" "the burial place of the Saints." William of Malmesbury describes it as "held in great reverence, on account of the number of Saints, Martyrs and Confessors, who had found a resting place, either by ending their days here, or whose bones, owing to its character for superior sanctity, had been translated hither . .. For it seems to have been the custom at Glastonbury, in early ages, to place the relics of some saint in a magnificent shrine, to attract a multitude of worshippers ... It, with the venerated Vetusta Ecclesia, was called the "Tomb of the Saints."

When the cemetery was excavated by archaeologists, it was found to bear ample evidence of long and intensive use. Slab-lined graves of the earliest period were found packed together in an endeavour to obtain burial as near as possible to the oratories and tombs of the Saints. Gildas, the historian, ended his last days at Glastonbury, as did St. David. King Coel, or Hoel, the father of Queen Helena and grandfather of Constantine) was also laid to rest there. Twelve disciples of St. Philip are reported to be buried in this venerable cemetery.

The possibility of Mary having been brought to Britain by Joseph of Arimathea, and her spending her remaining years on earth here, would not be inconsistent with the last New Testament account we have of Mary. We know that Mary, after the Ascension, dwelt among the disciples. We also know that the disciples had to flee Jerusalem for their very lives. It is not unreasonable to assume, that Joseph, being both Mary's uncle by marriage (and thus her legal guardian) and a wealthy, influencial, provincial Roman Senator, would have been the logical choice to take and protect the Blessed Mary.

The Scriptural record tells us that as Jesus hung on the Cross He tenderly committed His mother into John's safekeeping, who led Mary away from the tragic scene before her Son expired. Speaking of John, the Scriptures read: "From that hour that disciple took her unto his own" (John 19:27) - "eis ta idia," "idia" is possessive pronoun. The word "home" (K.J.) is not in the original text; the translators added it.

Jesus definitely entrusted His mother to the care of John but the request did not necessarily mean that John would see her safely provided for. In any case, it seems quite reasonable to expect John to turn to Joseph of Arimathea for the necessary protection. One early document (Magna Glastoniensis Tabula, at Naworth Castle) bears this out. It reads: "St. John, while evangelizing Ephesus, made Joseph Paranymphos." (meaning Guardian)

According to one Tradition of Glastonbury, after Mary's death, a building of wattle construction, sixty feet in length and twenty-six feet wide (following the pattern of the Wilderness Tabernacle) was built over her home. This building became known as the "Lignea Basilica" or the "Vetusta Eccesia" and the "Ealdechurche" or "Old Church." (Later it was called the "Culdee Church" or "Church of the Refugees.") The existence of a mud and wattle church at Glastonbury is historically proven by two royal Charters which are still extant. Both were actually signed in the "Lignea Basilica" — one by King Ina, in A.D. 704, and the other by King Cnut in A.D. 1032.

We can believe that Joseph, after the death of Mary, decreed that the place where she was buried should be forever dedicated to the worship of Christ. Later, he and his disciples would live together there, as a community, to ensure the perpetuation of worship on this holy spot. Maelgwyn of Avalon, (or Melchinus) the uncle of St. David, in his "Historia de Rebus Britannicis (written about A.D. 540) wrote: "In this church they worshipped and taught the people the true Christian faith. After about fifteen years Mary died and was buried at Glastonbury. The disciples died in succession and were buried in the cemetery."

In another reference to Mary, Maelgwyn wrote: "The Isle of Avalon greedy of burials ... received thousands of sleepers, among whom Joseph de Marmore from Aramathea by name, entered his perpetual sleep. And he lies in a bifurcated line next the southern angle of the oratory made of circular wattles by 13 inhabitants of the place over the powerful adorable Virgin." In yet another reference to Mary, Maelgwyn wrote concerning the saints buried at Glastonbury: "who there awaited the day of resurrection under the protection of the Mother of God." The implication in both statements is that Mary, as well as the other disciples including Joseph, were buried under the wattle church. This would further explain why the ancient church was called "Mary's Chapel" as well as "St. Joseph's Chapel."

Malmesbury's "Acts of the Kings" (written about A.D. 1135) also contains an enigmatic statement that adds to the subtle suggestion that Mary is buried at Glastonbury. Speaking of Mary's Chapel: "The very floor, inlaid with polished stone, and the side of the altar itself above and beneath, are laden with the multitude of relics." (translated) Then follows these words: "where also one can notice in the pavement stones are carefully set side by side, either in triangularly or squarely and sealed with lead, under which I believe some sacred secret to be contained. I shall not be an injury to religion." (translated) It is intriguing to believe that the "secret" referred to the actual burial place of the Virgin Mary.

The Virgin Mary was deified by the Roman Catholic Church in A.D. 600. She is held in affectionate memory, but was never deified, by the British Church. Christ, alone, from the beginning and to date, is the only Deity of the Church. Mary is regarded as but an instrument in the Divine purpose of God. There is no passage in the Bible that shows that Jesus regarded His mother as Divine. On the occasion when His disciples told Him that His mother and brethren were present, He asked, "Who is My mother?" and gives the explanation. Naturally, He regarded her dearly.

PIETA BY MICHELANGELO - ROME

It is also well known that the Roman Catholic Church dedications to St. Mary did not begin before A.D. 1130; a rite not practiced by the British Church — the one exception being Mary's Chapel at Glastonbury over a thousand years earlier. Thus, this early dedication had to be for a reason other than deification. Perhaps this was a continuation of the tradition that Jesus, Himself, dedicated to His mother the little "temple" He had built with His own hands at Avalon.

The late Rev. Lionel Smithett Lewis, Vicar of Glastonbury, spent years researching the validity of traditions placing Jesus and His mother Mary in Britain. He points out the unique place of honor accorded to Glastonbury and the Virgin Mary, by the Roman Catholic Church from earliest times to date. He states: "No one better than they (the Roman Catholic Church) know the facts of her (Mary's) life, and no one better than they espouse them. And over the ages the holy ground at Glastonbury has been constantly referred to by them as "Our Lady's Dowry." As such it has always been recognized by the Roman Catholic Sisterhood, who never ceased to pray daily for this hallowed spot at Glastonbury — Our Lady's Dowry." Rev. Lewis may have had in mind the French convent in Alexandria, conducted by nuns who were members of the old French nobility. They taught that St. Joseph of Arimathea took the Blessed Virgin with him to Britain and that she died there.

When printing was invented, the first book to come off the press was the Bible. Soon afterwards, Wynkyn de Worde, printed the life story of St. Joseph and about the same time Richard Pynson (A.D. 1516-1520) printed two accounts of the Arimathean story, from old documents, one of which carried these interesting lines:

> *"Now here how Joseph came into Englande;*
> *But at that tyme it was called Brytayne.*
> *Then XV yere with our lady, as I understande,*
> *Joseph wayted styll to serve hyr he was fayne."*

The length of time (15 years) could be the number of years Joseph was Mary's Paranymphos (Bridesman - Guardian) — from A.D. 33 to 48. The old ecclesiastical records of Glastonbury, confirmed by many other ancient writers, also state that the Virgin Mary departed this life in the year A.D. 48. Several other early documents are reputed to bear this out. One being the Cotton MS. Titus and another the Novo Legend Anglo, by John Capgrave. (Principal of the Augustine Friars in England - A.D. 1466) Coinciding with this, the old Glastonbury Abbey records officially declare that St. Mary's Chapel (later erected over the Wattle Church) built by St. David, was raised over her remains. Melchinus, a native of Avalona, (known also as "Maelgwyn") Celtic bard, historian and philosopher, who lived about A.D. 450 wrote: "Ye ealde chyrche was built over the grave of the Blessed Mary."

The latter manuscript particularly informs us that John gave Mary into the trust of Joseph, under the peculiar title of being her "brides-man;" that he was present at her death, as were other apostles and disciples who came at her bidding to be by her side as Mary breathed her last.

Over the centuries many places have claimed to be Mary's resting-place. In more modern times, the Roman Catholic Church named the Chapel of the Dormiton, near Jerusalem as the site. There a ledge is pointed out where Mary's "Koimesis" (falling asleep) took place. However, it, nor other places in the East have withstood the probe of investigation. None of the Disciples of the Gospel mention her tomb. St. Jerome, recording the sacred places of the East during the fourth century A.D. (by special commission of the Church at Rome) makes no reference to the burial place of Mary. The logical reason is she was not interred in Judea, or in Rome.

The Gnostics, in the fourth century A.D., started a legend that St. Mary lived at Bethlehem after her son's death, till an angel came to say that she must die; that she was borne in a cloud to Jerusalem, and carried by the Apostles to Gethsemane, where her soul was received by St. Gabriel and carried to Paradise. The story continues that the Apostles bore her body to the valley of Jehosaphat and laid in a new tomb; that the Lord appeared, ordered St. Michael to bring her soul from Paradise, re-unite it to her body, which was entrusted to angels and carried to heaven.

St. Epiphanus, (A.D. 315-402) Bishop of Constantia or Salamis, denounced the story as "The whole thing is foolish and strange, and is a device and deceit of the devil." (Haer 89) The saintly (Pope) Gelasius condemned this assumption of Mary as heretical in the year A.D. 494. In spite of these rejections, the "Festival of the Assumption" was instituted by the Emperor Maurice at the beginning of the seventh century A.D. Charlemagne rejected it. His son Lewis accepted it in A.D. 818. Today, under August 15, it is found in the Roman Breviary.

In A.D. 166, Bishop Eluetherius, at the request of King Lucius of Britain, sent two legates (holy men) — Phaganus and Deruvianus — who baptized the King and his family, at Glastonbury. Upon discov-ering the abandoned wattle church constructed by Joseph and his companions and dedicated to Mary, these two holy men elected to stay and form a religious community. They lived there nine years, and in memory of the first twelve, chose twelve from their converts to dwell on the island, as anchorets, in the separate spots occupied by them. King Lucius confirmed to these twelve converts the grants of twelve portions of land for their sustenance and their successors, the number always being twelve.

The new community restored the Vetusta Ecclesia of the Virgin, which was fast falling into decay. Then, they added an oratory of stonework which they dedicated to Christ and the holy Apostles, Peter and Paul. Successive converts maintained the community and its buildings, doing such repairs and substitution of parts as required. For centuries the fame of the dedication of the Vetusta Ecclesia attracted settlers from the northern parts of Britain to inhabit the island. Pilgrims of all ranks, holy, learned, and pious, visited it.

St. Patrick, the patron saint of Ireland, visited Glastonbury about A.D. 433, where he found twelve hermits living apart, in huts. He taught them to live together, in common, and appointed himself their Abbot. He held the office of Abbot until his death in A.D. 472, at the great age of 111 years. His Irish mission lasted 47 years and for 39 years he was Abbot of Glastonbury. He is said to have been buried beside the altar in the Vetusta Ecclesia, on the south side. St. Benignus, St. Patrick's disciple and third successor to his Irish Episcopate, came to Glastonbury A.D. 460 and succeeded him as Abbot.

Another early name associated with the Vetusta Ecclesia is St. David, or Dewisant. (born about A.D. 520) His contemporaries were Cadoc, Padarn, Samson, Dochu, Teilo, Comgall, Brendon, Gildas and the Irish Finnian. One story related by Malmesbury, is that David came from Wales with seven bishops "of whom he was primate" to dedicate the Old Church to the Blessed Virgin Mary. On the night before the ceremony, Jesus appeared to David in a vision and said that he had already done so and he must not: "He Himself had long before dedicated the church in honor of His mother and the sacrament ought not be profaned by human repetition." However, David immediately set about building another church "lest they should seem to come out for naught." The new church was sort of a chancel to the east of the Old Church. (Quendam cancellum)

So as to not confuse his building with the Old Church, David set up a pillar to the north and in line with the east wall of the earlier building. On it was a brass plate, inscribed with a statement of the distance from the pillar to the center of the East wall. The pillar was reported as still standing under Henry VIII. The foundation of just such a pillar was found in A.D. 1931 by Dr. Armitage Robinson and the spot is marked today with an iron post and notice. David died around A.D. 589 and was buried in the grounds of his own monastery, although there is a story that his remains were later brought to Glastonbury as was the bodies of many saints.

In A.D. 708, King Ina (or Ine, the son of Kendred), of Wessex, presented his famous charter to the "Lignea Basilica," which reads in part: "To the ancient church, situate in the place called Glastonbury, which church the Great High Priest and Chiefest Minister, formerly through His own Ministry and that of angels, sanctified by many an unheard of miracle to Himself and the ever Virgin Mary, as was formerly revealed to St. David, do grant ..."

The "Great High Priest" and "Chiefest Minister" are clearly a reference to Christ, Himself, and this would seem to affirm that He personally ministered there. This is certainly a confirmation of our interpretation of the Gildas statement that Christ afforded His light and a knowledge of His precepts. The ancient church referred to by King Ina was, of course, the little wattle church built perhaps by Joseph of Arimathea. Today, the site is covered by the ruins of the 12th century Church of St. Mary, known as Mary's or the Lady's Chapel.

EXTERIOR OF MARY'S CHAPEL

MAJOR ECCLESIA

In A.D. 719, King Ina built another church. This was the "Major Ecclesia" of the Apostles Peter and Paul. It was much larger and more imposing and situated a short distance to the east of the Vetusta Ecclesia. William of Malmesbury mentions that several Basilicas stood in this place: "The first and oldest — that built by the twelve disciples of St. Phillip and St. James, stood west of all the others. The second was made by St. David, in honour of the Virgin Mary, at the east part of the oldest, after he had prepared a solemn dedication by our Lord Himself. The third was built by the twelve pious men from the north part of Britain; this also stood east of the Vetusta Ecclesia. The fourth and largest was constructed by King Ina, in honour of the Saviour and the Apostles Peter and Paul, for the soul of his brother Mules; this, the Major Ecclesia stood east of all the others, while the Vetusta Ecclesia stood west of all the others."

King Ina also founded a school, at Rome, for the education of British subjects. He instituted "Peter's pence," which he at first called, "King's Alms." He enjoined every subject who possessed in his home any one kind of goods to the value of twenty pence, that he should pay a penny to the Pope yearly on Lammas Day. (Festival of the wheat harvest) Ina assumed the habit of a monk in the year A.D. 726 and died about the year A.D. 728, in Rome. Ina's monastery maintained a great reputation until it (with many other monasteries) was ravaged and despoiled by the Danes in the 6th century, A.D.

The next worthy recorded in the Annals of Glastonbury Abbey was the great Englishman, Dunstan, whose posthumous fame caused large sums of money and gifts to flow into the Abbey coffers for centuries. According to the Anglo-Saxon Chronicle, Dunstan was born in A.D. 925 in the neighborhood of Glastonbury, probably at Baltonsborough, where a church is dedicated to him. He was educated (as a monk) at the Abbey achool, then a celebrated seminary of learning. He is said to have excelled in the arts of music, painting, and goldsmith's work.

About A.D. 943 (some records give A.D. 936) Dustan was appointed Abbot of Glastonbury by King Edmund, brother and successor to King Athelstan. Being a pupil of the Benedictines (favored by Edmund) Dunstan established Glastonbury as the first Benedictine monastery in England. King Edmund's reign was short; he was murdered at Pucklechurch by Leofa, a robber, (A.D. 946) and was interred at Glastonbury by Abbot Dunstan. King Edred succeeded Edmund and during his nine year reign the Abbey prospered. Dunstan became the King's chief Minister as well as Abbot of Glastonbury. He seems to have hated the married state, perhaps influenced by his own disappointment as a young man. By instituting celibacy for the clergy, which had not yet become a dogma of the Church of Rome, Dunstan made many enemies among the married clergy.

St Dunstan, the Somerset- born ecclesiastical reformer, abbot of Glastonbury (from 945) and archbishop of Canterbury (960–988), abases himself at Christ's feet; detail from a tenth-century MS

On the death of **King** Edred (A.D. 955) his nephew Edwy (King Edmund's son) succeeded to the throne. He soon quarrelled wih Abbot Dunstan, who had reproved him for an illegal marriage. The King had Dunstan banished from the kingdom. He did not remain long abroad; for when the unpopular King Edwy's subjects deposed him and chose his brother Edgar to be King, Dunstan was recalled from exile. King Edgar appointed him Bishop of Worcester, A.D. 957, and in A.D. 958 Bishop of London. (Ref. Roger of Wendover) In the following year, Dunstan was elected Archbishop of Carterbury. He died in A.D. 988 and was buried at Glastonbury.

In A.D. 1082, Ailnothus (or Egelnoth) the last of the Saxon Abbots was replaced by a Norman Abbot named "Turstinus" or "Thurstan." The year following his installation, Thurstan had an aggravated quarrel with his monks who refused to accept some changes. The new Abbot wanted to substitute the chant of William of Fescamp for the Gregorian. (Anglo -Saxon Chronicle- A.D. 1083) The dispute ran so high that the Abbot called in armed bowmen to force the monks to obey. Some of the monks took refuge in the Great Church, but this sacred spot did not protect them. Several monks were killed and many wounded. The Anglo-Saxon Chronicle of A.D. 1083 records how "arrows stuck in the crucifix which stood above the altar ... and then wretched monks lay around the altar and some crept under it ... and blood ran on the steps."

Thurstan, after the custom of the Norman Abbots, commenced rebuilding the Great Church in the more ornate style. His successor, Abbot Herlewinus (in A.D. 1101) however, pulled down most of the Church started by Thurstan for the reason that he did not think it was grand enough for the magnitude of the revenues pouring into the Abbey. Succeeding Abbots continued to build and rebuild the great Church, always keeping the Vetusta Ecclesia separate from the Major Ecclesia. The most noted of these rebuildings took place under the direction of Henry of Blois, appointed Abbot in A.D. 1126, by his brother King Stephen.

According to Adam of Domerham, Henry, "he built this monastery from the foundation, a bell-tower, a chapter-house, cloister, lavatory, refectory, dormitory, and infirmary with a chapel; a splendid large palace; an exterior gateway of squared stones; a large brewhouse and stabling for many horses; giving many ornaments to the Church." (probably the church built by Abbot Herlewin) Henry found the precious Sapphire Altar (bestowed on Glastonbury by St. David) hidden in a recess in the Church of St. Mary, from the time of the wars with the Danes. He had it magnificently adorned with gold, silver and precious stones. This consecrated portable Sapphire Altar had been presented to St. David by the Patriarch of Jerusalem, with other costly gifts, when he visited the Holy City. Henry de Bois died in A.D. 1171 and was succeeded by Abbot Robert who ruled the Abbey for seven years. Following his death, King Henry II held the Abbey in his own hands, (no Abbot being appointed until A.D. 1189) entrusting the management of it to his chamberlain, Peter Marci, a Cluniac monk.

In A.D. 1184, a great fire, occurred, which consumed the greater part of the Glastonbury Abbey, including the venerable Wattle Church. Adam of Domerham gives the following account: "In the following summer, that is to say St. Urban's Day, (May 24, 1184) the whole of the Monastery, except a chamber with a chapel constructed by Abbot Robert (1178-9) into which the monks afterwards betook themselves, and the Bell Tower, built by Bishop Henry, was consumed by fire." No reason is given for the cause of the fire, but it is believed to have started from curtains ignited by candles during a wind storm.

Adam also recorded these moving words: "The beautiful buildings, lately erected by Henry of Blois, and the Church, a place so venerated by all, and the shelter of so many saints, are reduced to a heap of ashes! What groans, what tears, what pains arose as they (the monks) saw what had happened and pondered over the loss they had suffered. The confusion into which their relics were thrown, the loss of treasure, not only in gold and silver, but in stuffs and silks, in books and the rest of the ornaments of the church, must even provoke to tears, and justly so, those who far away do but hear of these things".

The greatest loss, however, was the famous library, considered the finest collection of books of the period, including records covering a thousand years of Glastonbury Abbey history. In the years preceeding its destruction, a large number of monks were constantly employed in the Abbey cloisters illuminating missals and transcribing, not only works of theology and devotion but of classical and general literature. Many of the books were illuminated on vellum (parchment) bound in richly tooled leather and mounted with silver and gold. Leland, who visited the library shortly before the great fire, wrote he was so overwhelmed with awe at the sight of such vast treasures of antiquity that for a time he dared not enter. Among the books and records, may have been the writings of those who had personally known Joseph, and perhaps Jesus during His sojourn in Avalon before His ministry.

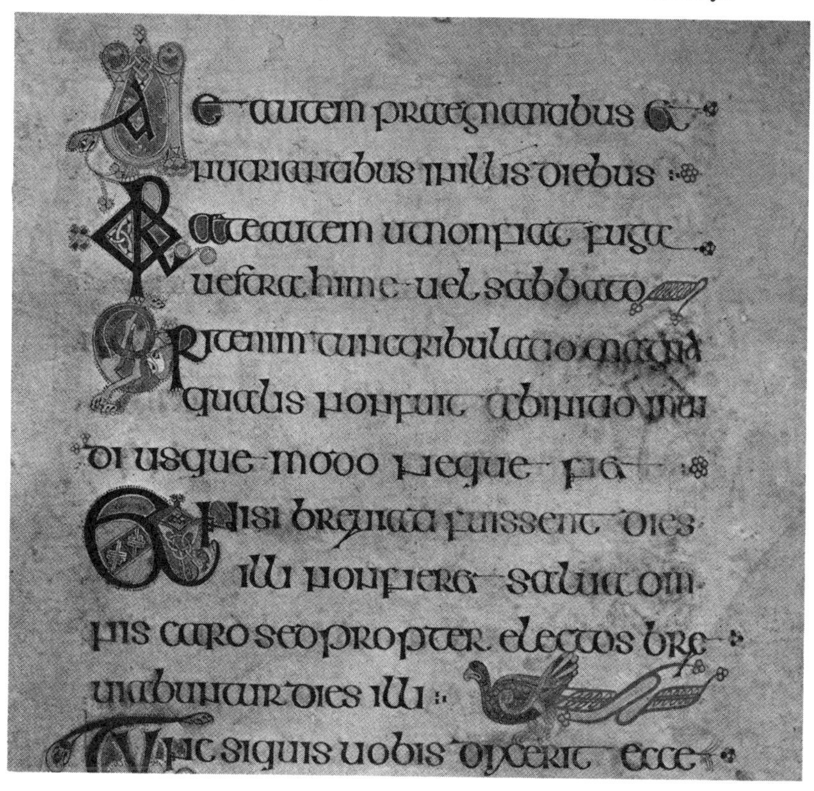
Uae autem praegnantibus et
nutrientibus in illis diebus
Orate autem ut non fiat fuga
uestra hieme uel sabbato
Erit enim tunc tribulatio magna
qualis non fuit ab initio mun
di usque modo neque fiet
Et nisi breuiata fuissent dies
illi non fieret salua om
nis caro sed propter electos bre
uiabuntur dies illi
Tunc si quis uobis dixerit ecce

A page of text, Matthew 24: 19-24, wherein Jesus foretells the events and trials of the last days. Typically, the fanciful decorative illuminations have little, if any, bearing on what is described in the text.

ILLUMINATED BOOK COVER

The four symbols of the evangelists. Conception comes from vision of Ezekiel of a cloud of fire containing four figures, each with face of a man but also appearing as a lion, ox and eagle.

Matthew was identified with man (upper left); Mark as lion (upper right); Luke as calf (lower left); John as eagle (lower right). The figures were also interpreted as four stages in the life of Christ.

SKETCH OF GLASTONBURY ABBEY AS IT APPEARED BEFORE ITS DESTRUCTION IN A.D. 1539

12th CENTURY ABBEY OF GLASTONBURY

King Henry II did not allow the Abbey to remain in ruins. He immediately issued a Royal Charter to rebuild, declaring that "because whatsoever a man soweth that shall he also reap." This meant that since the Church was reduced to ashes while in his hands, he, or his heirs, God willing, should magnificently complete the rebuilding of the Church of Glastonbury. Henry entrusted the work of rebuilding to his Chamberlain, Radulphus, the son of King Stephen. Radulphus first built the Church of St. Mary, "in the place where, from the beginning, the Vetusta had stood, with squared stones of the most perfect workmanship, profusely ornamented." The walls were supposed to have been built outside those of the earlier building so as to enclose it, and the remains of the older building were not removed until the walls of the latter were completed.

The Church of St. Mary, (known as Mary's Chapel or St. Joseph's Chapel) the most perfect of the ecclesiastical ruins of Glastonbury Abbey was built in the late transitional (Norman) style of architecture and remains to this day an admirable specimen of medieval masonry. Ornamentation consists of wide expanses of fine ashlar masonry and running patterns of foliage and tendrils, containing painted sun and stars. The flooring was composed of encaustic tiles (color being fused on with hot irons). Three of the walls are still standing and in the north and south walls are four, round-headed richly moulded windows, mullioned and rising nearly to the vaulting. A beautiful triple window at the west end, added light to the Chapel. The overall dimensions of the Chapel was 55 feet in length and 24½ feet in width. The Lady Chapel was finished and dedicated on St. Barnabas's day (June 11, 1186) by Reginal, Bishop of Bath.

EXTERIOR OF MARY'S CHAPEL

NORTH DOORWAY OF MARY'S CHAPEL

The Chapel was originally a detached building, with a turret at each corner. At present, two of these turrets remain. When the larger building (St. Peter and St. Paul) was built east of the Lady Chapel, a flight of stairs, extending across the building from wall to wall, was constructed to provide access to the Galilee (porch) which formed a junction between the two buildings. Two richly carved doorways occupy bays, north and south, the south door opened up to the monk's churchyard. Over the doorways are sculptures, illustrating Biblical scenes.

Unfortunately, the sculptures decorating these beautiful Norman doorways are in a very dilapidated state, making it difficult to decipher them. Our best interpretations from a paper read before the Somerset Archaeological Society at Wells in 1888, by Mr. Hope. He describes the four arches of the north doors as "No. 1, the inner and No. 3 as resting (each) on the jamb shafts, while No. 2 and No. 4 are continous bands springing from the ground round the arch, and reaching the ground again." The figures on the bands are:

Band No. 1 - Beginning from the left:

1. A woman kneeling (The Annunciation)
2. An angel (The Annunciation)
3. Two women embracing (The Salutation)
4. A large group, under arches, denoting a house with a bed in the center, with a sitting figure at the head. (The Nativity) The sitting figure being Joseph, with the Virgin and child in the bed. The broken section probably contained the ox and ass on the right.
5. A large group difficult to make out. On the left is a figure sitting with his back to, but his face turned to, an angel with outstretched wings. On the right of the angel is a small barefooted figure, and beyond a large figure.
6. 7. 8. Standing figures, all crowned, evidently the three kings asking of Herod, "Where is he that is born 'King of the Jews!'

Band No. 2 and No. 4 - are filled with miscellaneous figures and things pertaining to agriculture and life of the time and neighbourhood.

Band No. 3 - consists of 18 loops, containing:

1. A king standing (much broken) (A Magi)
2. A standing figure (head gone) (A Magi)
3. A man kneeling on one knee (A Magi)
4. Our Lady and Child, sitting (Receiving gifts from the Magi)
5. 6. 7. Each of these loops contains a mounted figure riding away, that is, the three Kings (Magi) going home.

8. 9. 10. Each contains a bed with a man asleep, with clouds above — Over 8. an angel issues from the clouds. This is the old way of depicting a vision, and represents the three kings being warned to return to their own country by another way.
11. An armed figure holding a shield and club or mace.
12. A king sitting.
13. A knight in chain mail striking at some object on his left or in his hand.
14. A knight in chain mail, with an infant impaled on his sword. (These last four loops depict the Massacre of the Innocents)
15. Two women weeping (In Ramah was a voice heard, lamentations and weeping)
16. A man in bed, the hand of God issuing from a cloud above (Joseph warned of the death of Herod)
17. An animal, broken, (but clearly the Return from Egypt)
18. A man carrying luggage (Joseph)
19. 20. (These last two loops are part of one subject)

Reginald (Bishop of Bath) laid out the foundations of the new Major Ecclesia. Its dimensions were 400 feet in length and 80 feet in width. The Chronicler Adam de Domerham, who continued William of Malmesbury's history of Glastonbury to the year A.D. 1290, narrates that "the stones of the great palace, built by Bishop Henry, also the entire wall which surrounded the monastery were used in the foundation, and that a "great part of the Major Ecclesia (Great Church) having been built, the remainder would have been completed, had the King's life been spared." Unfortunately, Henry II died in A.D. 1189, just five years after the foundations of the Church had been laid. Henry's son and successor, Richard Coeur de Lion (Richard the Lion Hearted) was too taken up by his great crusade to continue the building. Funds, once allocated for building the Abbey were diverted for other purposes. The monks tried to raise money by various means but were not successful. The rebuilding progressed slowly and at times stood still entirely. It was more than one hundred years before the work of the great Church was completed. Then, in A.D. 1275, years of work was destroyed by an earthquake that severely damaged the walls, necessitating replacement of many stones.

(Author's note: The following pages describing the rebuilding of Glastonbury Abbey is incomplete. Only some of the more noted Abbot's and their work are given. For a complete list of Abbot's of Glastonbury see Appendix B)

The work of rebuilding the Great Church, according to ecclesiastical building custom of the period commenced at the east end and continued westward until its junction with St. Mary's Chapel. (also known as St. Joseph's Chapel) Its plan represented a "cruciform" church, bays forming the arms of a cross, and square at the east end. The Nave consisted of ten bays. At first, the Choir consisted of four bays but was increased to six bays by Abbot Monington (A.D. 1371-1374); copied after the Choir at Wells Cathedral, which in the first half of the 14th century had been lengthened from three to six bays.

THE TRANSEPT OF THE ABBEY

The side-aisle walls of the Abbey extended two bays beyond the eastern gable, and continued at the back of it, thus forming the retro or processional aisle. Abbot Fromont (A.D. 1303-1322) commenced the Great Hall of the Abbey which was completed by Abbot Monington who partly rebuilt the Chapter House. This was, in turn, completed by his successor, Abbot Chinnock. Abbot Adam de Sodbury (A.D. 1322-1325) "vaulted nearly all the Nave and ornamented it with splendid paintings. He gave the great Clock, (now in Wells Cathedral) and also organs of wonderful magnitude. He endowed the Lady Chapel with four additional priests. He decorated the high altar with an image of the Virgin in the tabernacle of the highest workmanship."

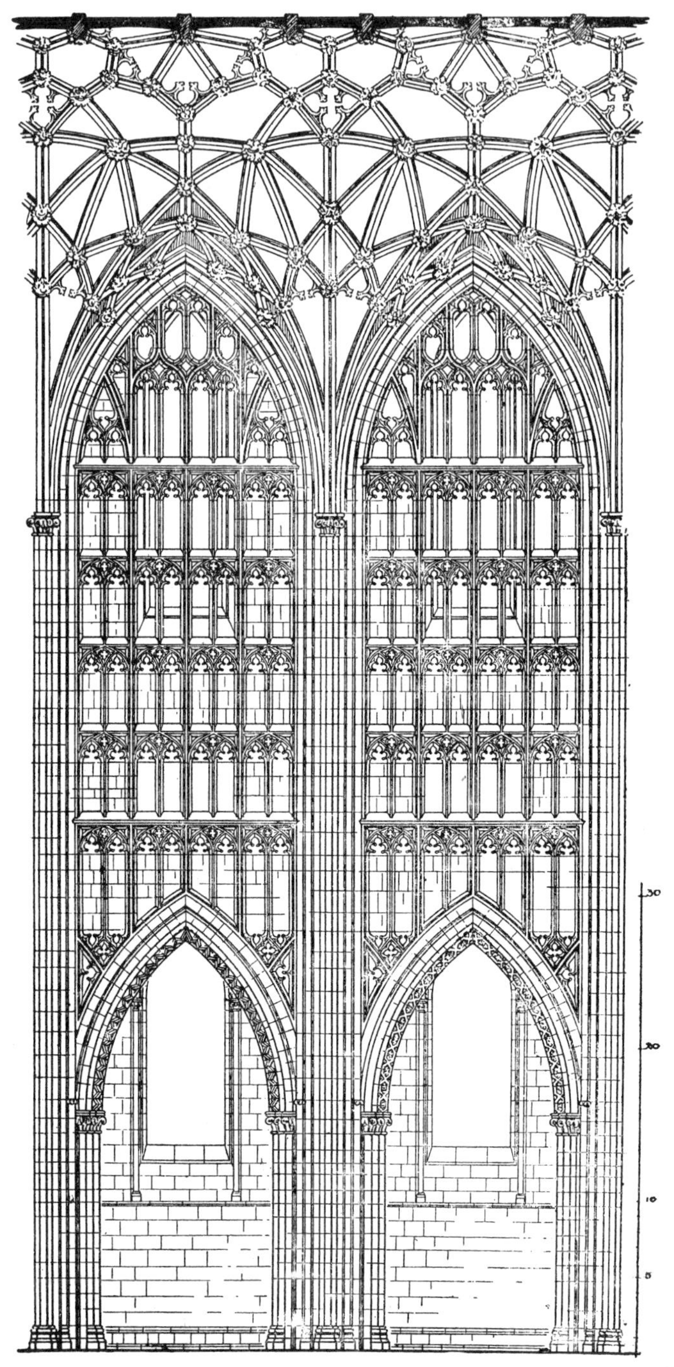

CONJECTURAL ELEVATION OF TWO BAYS OF ABBOT MONINGTON'S CHOIR

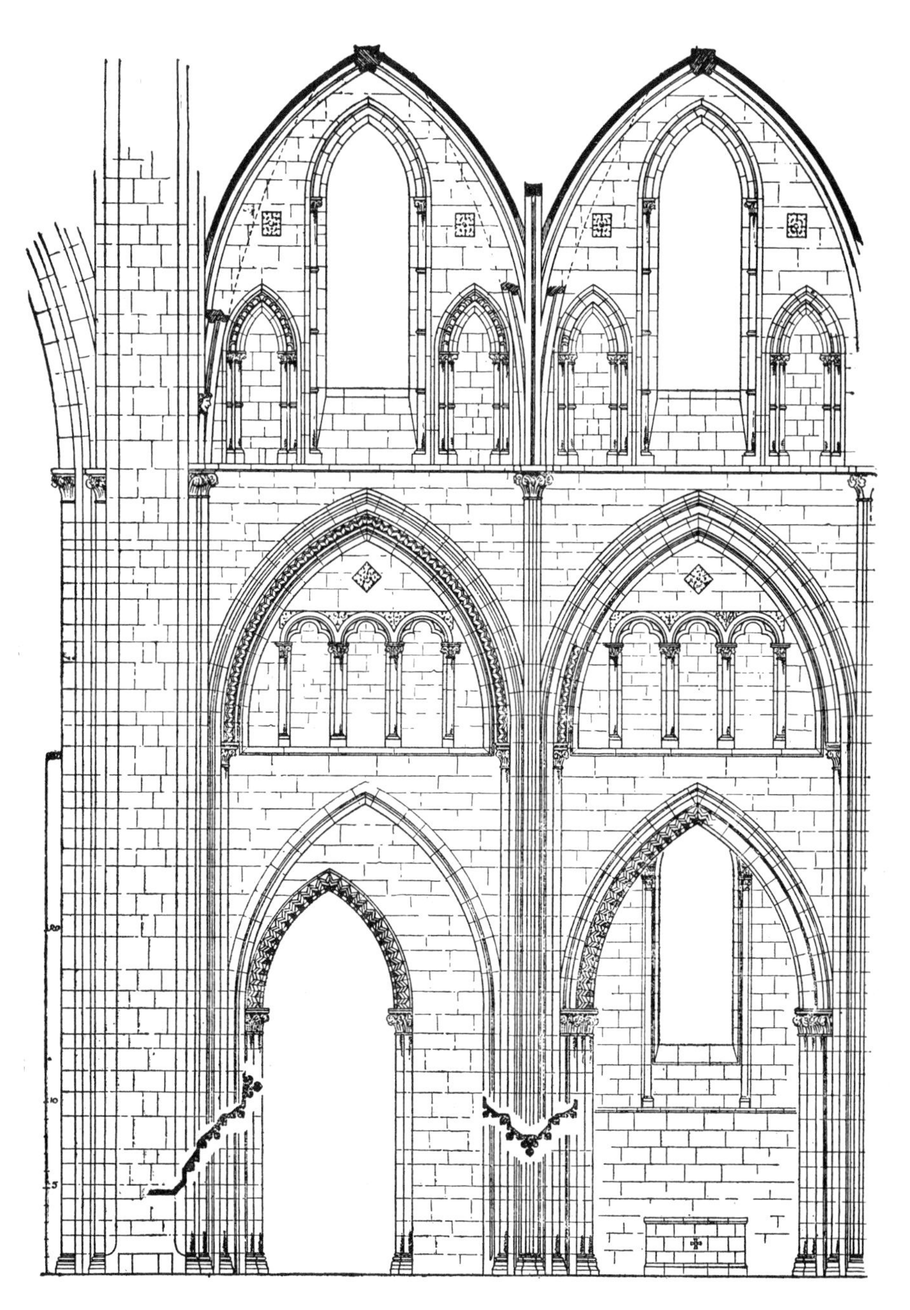

CONJECTURAL RECONSTRUCTION OF THE GLASTONBURY ABBEY SOUTH TRANSEPT AND CROSSING OF THE ABBEY (13th CENTURY)

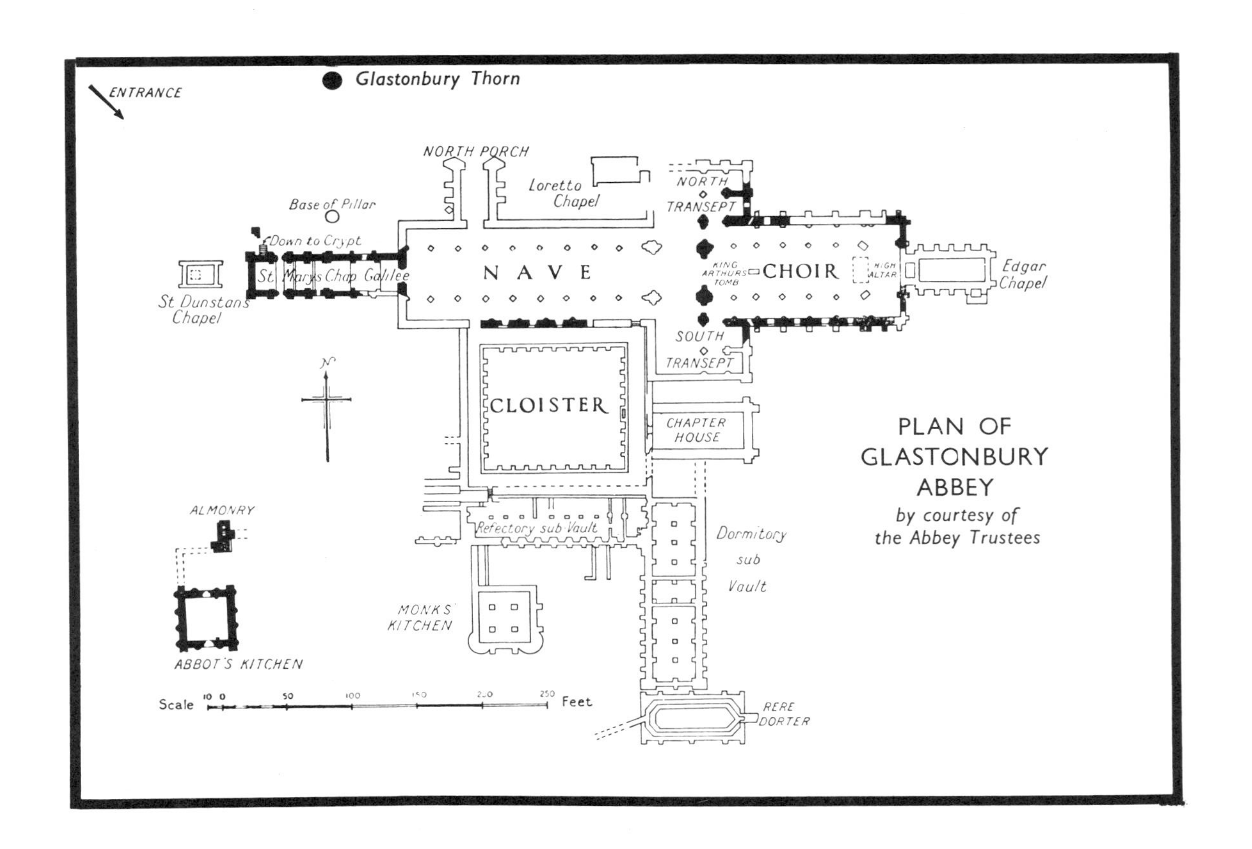
ENTRANCE
Glastonbury Thorn
NORTH PORCH
Loretto Chapel
NORTH TRANSEPT
Base of Pillar
Down to Crypt
St Marys Chap
Galilee
NAVE
KING ARTHURS TOMB
HIGH ALTAR
CHOIR
Edgar Chapel
St Dunstans Chapel
SOUTH TRANSEPT
CLOISTER
CHAPTER HOUSE
PLAN OF GLASTONBURY ABBEY
by courtesy of the Abbey Trustees
ALMONRY
Refectory sub Vault
Dormitory sub Vault
MONKS' KITCHEN
ABBOT'S KITCHEN
RERE DORTER
Scale
Feet

It is believed that the great "Clock" given to the Abbey by Adam de Sodbury, was made by a Glastonbury monk by the name of Peter Lightfoot. (Lightfote) John Leland, writing in A.D. 1539, says of a clock which he saw at Glastonbury: "Peter Lightfote, the monk made this clock." The clock was placed in the South Transept of the Abbey. At the dissolution of the Abbey in A.D. 1529, the clock with its automatic mechanism, was carried toWells and placed in the North Transept of the Cathedral. The works have been renewed several times, but it is the oldest known clock, self-striking the hours with a count wheel.

The dial plate is six and a half feet in diameter, contained in a square frame, having the figure of an angel holding a man's head puffing, in each corner. The outer figure is divided into 24 parts, representing the 24 hours in a day. The numbers are in Old English characters, and mark the hours from twelve at noon to mid-night, and then to twelve at mid-day. A large gilt star points to the hour. An inner or second circle shows the minutes, and a small star moves around the circle every hour. A third circle gives the age of the moon. A plate in this circle shows the moon. There is also a smaller circle in which there is a female figure, having around it the motto, "Semper peregrat Phoebe." (So progresses Phoebe) Above the dial plate is a panelled tower, around which four Knights on horseback revolve in opposite directions every hour on the striking of the clock. They represent a mimic tournament.

The Knights rush around with such ferocity that one unfortunate is felled at each encounter, and he has barely time to recover his upright position before he is again knocked down with resounding clatter upon his horse's back. (On passing behind the turret the smitten Knight is automatically set up again, only to receive another "knock-out blow," and so on, in rapid succession during several encounters, with a most comic effect) The other three Knights fight twenty-four times a day unscathed.

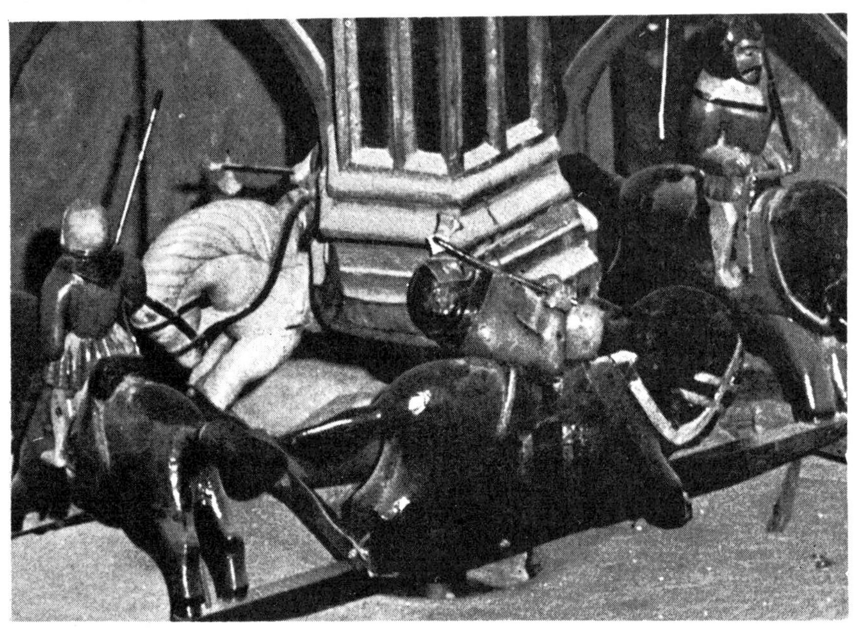

A figure in the costume of King Charles I (which may have replaced one of more ancient date) is seated some distance from the clock at a higher elevation. The figure strikes with its heels against bells; two strokes at the quarter hour; four strokes at the half hour; six strokes at the third quarter; eight strokes at the hour. It also strikes with a hammer on a bell the number of the hour.

One inscription on the clock gives the key to the whole clock-face. Around the moon plate are the words: "Sphericus archetypum globus hic monstrat micracosmum" which is translated, "This circular (rounded) dial represents the actual universe in miniature." This accounts for the sun and stars, the moon, and the earth in the center, (as it was then visualized). The figures of angels, each holding a man's head puffing, represents the four cardinal winds.

To summarize the astronomical aspect of the clock, we have the Earth at the center, with the Moon revolving round it in strict accordance with the Ptolemaic conceptions of the diurnal (daily happenings) and proper motions; the sun making its journey round the Earth once in 24 hours; the starry firmament outside these and the four cardinal winds in their traditional places at the corners. Lightfoot's clock, then is not merely a clock but is essentially a model illustrating fundamental Medieval conceptions of creation and the Universe. It is remarkable that a simple monk of the Glastonbury Abbey had the ingenuity and skill to devise and construct a clock of this kind.

Abbot Breynton(A.D. 1335-1341) built the Prior's Hall, (Refectory) the Kitchen, the steps which led up to the orchard, and commenced building the Abbot's Chapel which was completed by Abbot Selwood, (died A.D. 1493). Abbot Chinnock (A.D. 1374-1420) rebuilt the Cloister which had been allowed to fall into disrepair, the Dormitory and the Fratery. He was interred in the Chapter House which he had finished. Abbot Beere (A.D. 1493-1524) ruled the Abbey for thirty-one years. He excavated the Crypt of Mary's Chapel and raised the floor to seat-level. He also added the tracery to the windows. In addition, he built the Loretto Chapel, the Chapel of the Sepulcher, part of the Edgar Chapel, (which was completed by his successor, Abbot Whiting) and "built the lodgings by the great chamber called the 'King's Lodging' for secular priests and clerks of our Lady."

The Crypt in Mary's Chapel was excavated to provide burial space for the faithful within the walls of the Chapel. The desire of those who could pay for the privilege of finding final resting place in the immediate vicinity of where Joseph (and perhaps Mary, herself) ever increased as time went on. Lead from the crowned coffins there, less than a hundred years later, formed part of the spoil of the destroyers. The excavation extended from the foot of the steps which lead into the great Church, (but not carried under them) the whole length of the Chapel from east to west. The extreme thickness of the walls (six feet and the depth of the foundations over twelve feet) allowed the Crypt to be excavated to a depth of eleven feet.

A perpendicular doorway at the north west corner led into the Crypt. In 1825, Mr. John Fry Reeves, the then owner of the Abbey grounds had the Crypt cleared out. He found the steps ruined. In order to effect a better entrance he cleared a passage some yards to the north. In making the necessary excavations "eighteen coffins were found, all placed east and west. The length of one was eight feet three inches inside. The whole length of it was filled by a skeleton. All coffins were made of oak, two to three inches thick. Under the head and shoulders of each corpse was placed a bundle of wood shavings. Beneath, and on the right side of each skeleton, was a rod or thorn (or hazel) of the same length as the coffin."

On the south side of the Crypt is an arched recess; the following description of its discovery appears in "Warner's Glastonbury." (Ibid, p. 29). "The Holy Well was discovered in 1825 in searching for hidden antiquities, by a party of gentlemen. In the crypt, then choked up with rubbish, they sank a pit, when their progress was arrested by a mass of stonework; this was found to be the crown of the arch; the labour of a few hours detected a flight of steps leading to this subterraneous recess, uncovered a pavement, at the depth of ten or twelve feet from

INTERIOR OF MARY'S CHAPEL

the surface, and displayed a small well, overhung, and protected by the arch above it. Admeasurement of chamber and well — length of recess, seventeen feet — diameter of the well, two feet, two inches — depth, four feet, nine inches; an ornamental scroll decorates the arch of the recess."

THE HOLY WELL

The Well is outside the foundation wall of the Chapel, and as old, at least, as the Chapel itself. The round-headed arch of the recess is ornamented with a zig-zag scroll of the same character as that which so beautifully decorates the ruins of the Chapel. Opposite the Well there is a singular stair of five steps; these lead, by a passage to a flight of steps in the thickness of the wall, to a low doorway through an arcade. The doorway must have led to a small chapel which stood on the south side of the Lady Chapel; traces of its abutment upon the outside wall of the Chapel are plainly visible.

GLASTONBURY ABBEY FROM PRINT BY CONEY (1817)

THE DISSOLUTION OF THE GLASTONBURY MONASTERY

In A.D. 1524, the last Abbot, Richard Whiting was appointed. He had the unfortunate fate to be caught up in the tumult of the Dissolution of the Monasteries under King Henry VIII. In the twenty-sixth year of King Henry's reign (A.D. 1535) when the king had been declared "Supreme head of the Church," Abbot Whiting, at the head of his monks, signed the deed and thus showed his obedience to the King. Afterwards, when called upon to surrender his monastery, he preemptorily refused to do so as being against his conscience. In September A.D. 1539, three commissioners were sent by the King to inspect the Abbey. In the library they found a book opposed to Henry's divorce and the oath of supremacy was then offered to the Abbot. Whiting refused to take the oath and was taken to the Tower of London for further questioning by Cardinal Wolsey.

While Abbot Whiting was incarcerated another examination of the monastery was made. This time a gold chalice and other plate was found hidden by the Abbot that had not been shown to the commissioners. This was considered "the very high and rank treasons" and the Abbot remained imprisoned until November 14th, when he was taken back to Wells, Somerset for trial Whiting was convicted with two other monks and they were sentenced to be hanged. The order, attributed to Thomas Cromwell read: "Item, the Abbot of Glaston to be tried at Glaston and also to be executed there," (Remembrances — Cromwell) that is, re-tried. The next day, they were all drawn on hurdles to the Tor, hanged, disembowelled, beheaded, and quartered. The poor old Abbot's white head was set over the gate, and his quarters, boiled in pitch, were displayed at Well, Bath, Iichester, and Bridgwater.

At Abbot Whiting's death, (A.D. 1539) the Abbey came into the King's possession. The lands were divided and sold; the monks and the servants dismissed; the holy relics and treasures sent in bags to the King. The buildings were then broken up and sold in pieces. The destruction of Roche Abbey (described by eyewitnesses of the fate) may tell us of the fate of the Glastonbury Abbey:

"Some took the Service Books that lied in the Church, and laid them upon their waine coppes to piece the same: some took windows of the Haylath, and hid them in their hay; and likewise they did of many other things; for some pulled forth iron hooks out of the walles that brought none, when the yeomen and gentlemen of the country had bought the timber of the church. For the church was the first thing that was put to the spoil; and then the Abbot's lodging, dorter, and Frater, with the cloister and all the buildings thereabouts; for nothing was spared, but the ox-houses and swine-coates, and such other houses of office, that stood without the walls; which had more favour showed them than the very church itself: which was done by the advice of Cromwell, as Fox reporteth in his Book of Acts and Monuments."

While the ruthless destruction of the Abbeys is appalling and the sacredness of human life ignored, one should not lose all sense of proportion and sound judgement concerning the necessity of the Reformation. Britain had to have a man like Henry VIII because she had a king like Ina, who surrendered the Abbeys to a Roman Pope. It is impossible for us to know through what persons, or in what manner, God will at any time act, though it is obvious that He is acting. Henry VIII was only a pawn in the hand of God, used to break down the old Roman Ecclessiastical order in Britain. Also, the arrogancy of some of the Abbots toward the people played no small part in the suppression of the monasteries.

Rev. L.S. Lewis, who wrote so learnedly and so well on Glastonbury, says: "We must come to the conclusion, while gratefully acknowledging the work of the monks here and elsewhere, so needed in their age, that had this great Abbey remained true to God and herself, had there been less quarreling, less greed, less haughtiness, and more simple religion, He would have guarded it to this day." (Glastonbury — Her Saints, pg. 30) And on pg. 66, Lewis adds: "The Abbeys were to reap the whirlwind of their faults." It should be added that by contrast to other Abbeys of the period, the Glastonbury Abbey was well managed and loved by the people under its jurisdiction.

To fully understand the Monastic system one must be brought face to face with the spectacle of the Abbeys in the 14th and 15th centuries. They were rich in worldly possessions, as glorious in architectural splendor. The Benedictine monks had foresworn the world, only to repossess its luxuries under more assured condition. When Henry VIII came, they had become so drugged with the rich poisonous wines of enjoyment that not only the monks but many Abbots themselves turned thieves and common pilferers. Many of the Abbey treasurers were deliberately stolen, hidden away, or sold by the prior ascetics who had voluntarily taken the vows of poverty and sanctity.

A 19th century antiquarian standing in the ruins of the Glastonbury Abbey, reflecting on its past glories wrote: "History pictures the shadowy aisles filled with the pomp and splendor of those bygone ceremonies with the long procession of the monks with the kingly Abbot, who as he swept in state from his monastery along the cloistered walk, could rest his eye on a fair and smiling country, which as far as he could see, was all his own. As the choir-boys' chorals smote his ear, heaven and earth must indeed have seemed to clap their hands for joy over so royal a possession. Perhaps, if the sons of heaven had less interest in fat living and not attempted to appropriate so much of earth, the swift-footed Nemesis of the Reformation might have stayed its speed ... It is a pity that these brethren could not have gone out in a greater blaze of glory." (Cathedral Days - A.B. Dodd)

RUINS OF THE GREAT CHURCH OF ST. PETER AND ST. PAUL

VIEW OF GLASTONBURY ABBEY RUINS IN 1723
(FROM STUKELEY'S ITINERARY)

For over two hundred years, the Abbey served as a quarry for desecrating builders. Half of Glastonbury town, as well as the long causeway across the Sedgemoor, has been constructed out of its fallen mass of ruins. Stones were taken for the erection of walls, sheds, farm buildings, etc. Thus, the Abbey stone is scattered over a radius of many miles from the town. The excellent squared freestone proved a most tempting spoil for the house-builders, who also found use for the rubble core of the walls and the heavy stonework of the foundations.

The Cannon M.S. gives the lamentable record of one vandal tenant of the Abbey as "one Thomas Prew, a rank presbiterian, who pull'd down and sold vast quantities of ye stones, and rooted up ye vaults by blowing them up with gunpowder. He also pull'd down ye ancient Hall, and with the stones built a dwelling-house near ye gate called Magdalen's Gate, and placed in ye front and walls, ye arms, cyphers, and other decorations figures of ye Abbots, Priors, etc. ... and escutcheons which was once in ye old buildings, and many other stones he sold to amend ye roads and highways and to ye Townspeople with wch many houses have been built, and it was observable yt such houses so built, did not long stand, nor the possessors thrive."

RUINS OF THE GREAT CHURCH OF ST. PETER AND ST. PAUL
GLASTONBURY

A final period of destruction was inaugurated by one John Down, also a Presbyterian, who held the Abbey for sixty years, during the latter part of the 18th and the first few decades of the 19th centuries. It was during his tenancy that the last trace of two small chapels, (Loretto and Edgar Chapels) including their foundations, disappeared. After the death of John Down, the Abbey passed into the hands of more reverent custodians. Since then, its history has been a more fortunate one. One owner, a Mr. Reeves, did much to preserve what was left. It was he who threw across the area of the crypt, of St. Mary's Chapel, the arches of plain stone. These arches have helped greatly to prevent the further subsidence of this structure after the fall of the vault. The fall happened in A.D. 1784, when practically the whole of the floor disappeared into the crypt below, and the vault was full of water.

One of the most unique monuments that remains from olden times is an ancient stone that silently stares down on beholder, from the standing outside south wall of the Lady or Mary's Chapel. This time and weather-worn tablet has puzzled scholars for centuries. It bears but two names: "Jesus" — "Maria." (The Lombardic lettering is 13th century) Devoid of any other markings with a definite meaning, it has all the hallmarks of a very ancient piece of masonry, preserved from the disastrous fire of A.D. 1184. The question is often asked by visitors, "Why was it put there?" — "What does it mean?"

STONE IN SOUTH WALL OF MARY'S CHAPEL

Rev. Lewis gives a plausible answer: "It represents the signature of Jesus, naming the Dowry He had provided for His mother Mary." He goes on to explain that the title "Domus Dei" or "House of God" (attached to the Chapel) represents the Wattle Church or Temple, because therein He dwelt. And "Secretum Domini" or "Secret of the Lord" also attached to the Chapel) was the Dowry and dedication of the same to His mother. In substance, the ancient stone registers the record and site of "Our Lady's Dowry." This same title is officially recorded in the historical Domesday Book and does substantiate this interpretation.

The Glastonbury Abbey estate of some forty acres was purchased in 1907 on behalf of the Church of England, by public subscription, at a cost of £ 36,000. The property is vested in the Bath and Wells Diocesan Trustees upon trusts declared in a trust document dated 6th June 1908. The estate comprises the ruins of the ancient Abbey; the Abbey House (now a Diocesan house of retreat, conference and study) and park lands; the Abbey gatehouse and three cottages.

On June 22, 1908, a Thanksgiving Service was held in the Glastonbury Abbey ruins. It was attended, on behalf of the Crown, by the Prince and Princess of Wales, later to become King George V and Queen Mary. The Archbishop of Canterbury (Dr. Davidson) and a large number of prelates and clergy took part. Since that day, an annual pilgrimage takes place there on the last Saturday in June. The ecclesiastical leaders of the English Church rededicate themselves to Christ at Glastonbury.

Today, having endured the weather, the storms, and the violence of many generations, Glastonbury Abbey still stands. Pilgrims from all corners of the world have visited and continue to visit this holy shrine. There can be no doubt that the Glastonbury Abbey is the oldest, continuous Christian foundation in the world. Since the time when Joseph built his first church on the Sacred Isle of Avalon, men have worshipped Christ on that site. The buildings may have changed, the ecclesiastical orders may have changed, but worship of the Lamb of God has never ceased at Glastonbury Abbey.

THE LITTLE THORNTREE

The little Thorntree cried and cried,
when men's hands stripped it bare,
They made a rough and cruel crown,
To put on Jesus' hair.

He died upon the rugged cross,
From sin to set us free,
The little Thorntree cried with shame.
That day on Calvary.

Then Joseph laid His body down,
The scripture to obey,
And from the Thorn he chose a branch.
To carry far away.

To Glastonbury's hilly land,
Upon its sacred mound'
He took the little Thorntree twig,
And put it in the ground.

It grew into a stately tree,
The pilgrims loved the sight,
To glory our dear Saviour's name,
It blooms each Christmas night.

Kirsten Parsons

THE HOLY THORN TREE

Perhaps the most dramatic of all the Traditions of Glastonbury is the legend of the Holy Thorn Tree. It is stated that when Joseph and the band of refugees first arrived on the Sacred Isle of Avalon, it was in December. (some legends say it was on Christmas day) Joseph thrust his staff (some authorities have suggested it was the staff of Christ Himself) in the ground, perhaps to signify his journey was over. To this day, the spot bears the name it received in Joseph's time — "Wyrall" or "Weary-all-Hill."

Shortly, the staff, in the moist ground, took root, budded and blossomed and eventually grew into the famous "Glastonbury Thorn." The Thorn has endured through the centuries as a phenomenon of nature. It is the only thorn tree in the world to bloom in December (around Christmas time) and again in the month of May. Modern botanists agree that the Glastonbury Thorn is a unique Levantine hawthorn, (Crataegus Monogyna Praecox) a native of countries bordering on the eastern Mediterranean Sea. Its leaves become thick and leathery, which is typical of many plants native to semi-desert regions. The tree tends to hold its leaves throughout the entire winter.

Some writers state the blooming of the Thorn Tree around Christmas time is in honor of Christ's birthday. However, one thing is certain, December 25th was not the birthday of Jesus. The latest Chronology gives September 29, 2 B.C. as the birthday of Jesus. The birthday of Jesus would never had been celebrated by Joseph of Arimathea and it was never observed by the early Christian Church. Long centuries before the Christian era, the 25th of December was celebrated as a pagan holiday in honor of Nimrod, the "virgin-born" son of Baal, the sun-god. His mother was worshipped as the "Queen of Heaven" with Nimrod as the (false) messiah. Eventually, this pagan holiday (Christmas Day) was incorporated into the Christian calendar with Christian overtones.

The Glastonbury Holy Thorn Tree is unique because it has no exact parallel among the native English trees, in its propensity to bloom twice each year. Noteworthy to the reader is that the natural blooming period of the Levatine (Palestine) thorn is during the month of December while the native thorn of Britain blossoms only in the month of May. The earliest documentation of the Holy Thorn Tree, coming into blossom at Christmas time, is given in the "life of Joseph of Arimathea," printed in A.D. 1520, by Richard Pynson. Thus, for over 400 years, the Holy Thorn Tree is known to have preserved its peculiar feature of flowering twice each year.

A local ballad says:

"The staff het budded and het grew,
An at Chursnas bloomed the whoe day droo;
An still het blooms Chursnas bright,
But best that zay at dark midnight."

During the ascendency of the fanatical element among the Puritans, the Holy Thorn Tree was cut down. Its executioners justified the vandalism by declaring that the Thorn Tree had become an object of idolatry. It is said the fanatic who wielded the axe was wounded by a thorn in the eye, losing its sight, for his efforts. It should be noted that the Puritans were men who were deeply in earnest about religion. Most of them quite genuinely believed that by removing images, and other objects of veneration, they were bringing the people nearer to God. In their misguided zeal many churches were despoiled; glass windows were smashed, carvings disfigued and frescoed paintings on walls were covered with thick coatings of whitewash.

METAL ENCLOSURE PROTECTS DESCENDANT OF THE ORIGINAL THORN

At the time of its destruction, the original Thorn was a gigantic tree for its species, and was in two main trunks. One was completely demolished and the other badly damaged, nearly cut through. It survived, in this condition, for about another thirty years. During this time numerous cuttings were taken from it. The trees grown from these cuttings continued the characteristics of the original, in that they blossom twice, around Christmas and again in May. This phenomenon is noted only in those trees budded or grafted from the original, or from a budded descendant.

Bishop Godfrey Goodman of Gloucester (A.D. 1583-1656) visited Glastonbury and observed the revived Holy Thorn Tree. He wrote: "The White Thorn of Glastonbury which usually blossom on Christmas day was cut down, yet I did not heare that the party was punished ... Certainly, the thorne was very extraordinary; for at my being there I did consider the place, how it was sheltered; I did consider the soile, and all othe circumstances, and yet I could find no natural cause."

About the end of the eighteenth century, a certain Jonathon Clarke had a stone marker carved and placed to mark the site of the original Holy Thorne Tree. It carries the inscription, "J.A., A.D. XXXI." The date of A.D. 31 is wrong as it was several years later before Joseph of Arimathea brought his little band of followers to Avalon.

THE HOLY THORN TREE OF GLASTONBURY ABBEY

In olden days, a spray of Glastonbury's flowering Holy Thorn Tree was always taken and presented to the King (or Queen) of England. The custom fell into disuse for a time but was reinstated by His majesty King George V. (A.D. 1865-1936) The present Queen Elizabeth II is now the recipient of this age-old custom. This legend of the Holy Thorn Tree was held in such strong faith that in olden days sailors carried pieces of it for protection. Men died in peace if they were assured that a spray would be buried with them.

Slips from the Holy Thorn Tree have been sent to many countries. In October 1901, six cuttings from the Glastonbury Abbey Thorn Tree were sent to the Rt. Rev. Henry Yates Saterlee, the first Bishop of Washington D.C., U.S.A. Two trees are known to have been grown from these cuttings. One is an enormous tree that can be seen on the close of Washington National Cathedral, where it grows in its own plot of ground in front of St. Albans School for boys. The other is growing in the Brooklyn Botanic Gardens: One famous descendant of the Holy Thorn Tree is in the courtyard of the home of Mary Queen of Scots, in St. Andrews, Scotland.

THE CHALICE WELL

It is quite significant that at the foot of Chalice Hill there is located a well that runs as a spring. Since earliest times it has been known by two names, "Chalice Well" and "Holy Well." The Well is fed by an underground river believed to originate in the Mendip Hills to the north. Its outflow is about 25,000 gallons of water daily, without regard to climatic fluctuations. It has a year around temperature of 10°C. Wonderful curative powers have been claimed for the water. On May 5, 1751, as many as 10,000 persons were drawn to the Well following a published account of a certain Matthew Chancellor of North Wooton, afflicted by asthma, who, "recovered of his disorder" after being directed to drink the water.

The Well, itself, is built of massive squared blocks of local lias stone and is orientated, roughly, north and south. The stones are put together in wedge-formation, forming two chambers; the inner one being reached through an opening at the foot of the western wall of the well shaft. The shaft is approximately 41 inches square and about 9 feet deep; the spring being in the center. What is noteworthy is that the lower five and a half feet of the well are apparently undisturbed, but above this the blocks project irregularily with cut-away and worn surfaces. This suggests that these upper stones are the remains of a corbelled roof. Above these stones, there are signs of the walls of the Well being heightened in more recent times.

It has been suggested that originally the well chamber had been above ground. But in the course of time, with rain and earthquakes in the 13th century, the chamber became silted over by soil from the hillside above. This belief was strengthened by excavations just east of the Well (in 1961) that uncovered the stump of a yew tree nearly 12 feet below the present surface. The tree had a fine tap-root and part of the trunk — in all some two and a half feet long. It was found in a layer of blue-grey clay, and clearly was "in situ" where it had formerly grown. A specimen was sent to Leeds University where it was tested for water content and found to have been a living tree in Roman times. (cir. A.D. 300) This would suggest that the ground level at that period was approximately the same as the present bottom of the Well and that the water came out as a surface spring.

It was also noted that the yew tree stump was in line with other yew trees growing near the Well and on two lower terraces of the slope. This led the archaeologists who uncovered the yew tree stump to believe that in ancient times a path came up from the valley to the Well along the line of yew trees. There is evidence that the Well was frequented from earliest times. The excavations produced several dozen flints (upper Paleolithic or Mesolithic) and a shard of Iron Age pottery — the first to be found outside the famous Lake Villages. Roman and medieval shards were also found in more recent layers.

The earliest record of the Well is in the writings of William of Malmesbury. He commented that the waters were sometimes blue and at other times red, so that Chalice Well possessed the alternative appellation of "Blood Spring." One of the Traditions of Glastonbury relates that Joseph of Arimathea hid the "Chalice" (Cup of the Last Supper) in the Well. According to legend, after doing so the waters streamed forth blood. The water does leave a crimson deposit on the stones over which it flows. But, the red hue is nothing more prosaic than the natural result of their being iron (chalybeate) in the water.

The legend of the "Blood Spring" is related to the tradition that when Joseph came to Britain with the Cup of the Last Supper, he also brought two "cruets" (small, stopped glass flagons) — one of them holding the blood, the other one the sweat of Jesus, washed from Our Saviour's wounded body after the Crucifixion. This tradition is commemorated on a white cloth in the east window of Langport Church, nine miles from Glastonbury.

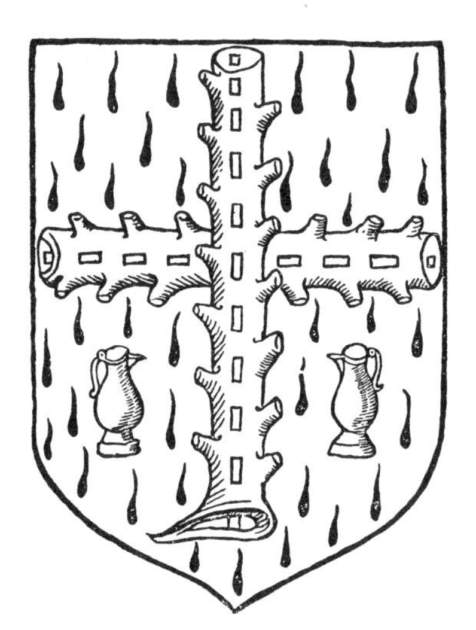

ARMS OF ST. JOSEPH OF ARIMATHEA

The traditions of the cruets may also be noted today on the hearaldic arms of the town of Glastonbury and on the Coat of Arms of Joseph of Arimathea. An example of Joseph's Coat of Arms can be seen in the south window of the 15th century Parish Church of Glastonbury. The more modern version of the Coat of Arms shows a chalice superimposed on a Holy Thorn cross, with the cruets omitted;

replaced by the original drops of blood, symbolizing the sorrow of the burial. The ancient histories of the life of St. Joseph, in Britain, make constant references to the Holy Cruets.

HERALDIC SHIELD BEARING A CROSS BETWEEN TWO CRUETS ON SHARPHAM MANOR HOUSE WALL NEAR GLASTONBURY

Maelgwyn of Avalon makes mention of the cruets as being buried with Joseph at Glastonbury: "Joseph had with him moreover in his sarcophagus, two white and silver cruets filled with the blood and sweat of the prophet Jesus. When his sarcophagus shall be opened it will be seen whole, and untouched in the future, and will be open to the whole world." (Historia de Rebus Brittannicis)

The present Well lid of wrough iron, patterned after a 13th century design, was presented as a "thank-offering gift for Peace," in 1919, from friends of the Chalice Well Trust. The Trust was founded by the late Major Wellesley Tudor Pole, O.B.E., in 1958, to preserve and safeguard for the public good, in perpetuity, the sanctity of the Chalice Well property. The design of the Well lid symbolizes the "Bleeding Lance" and the "Visible" and "Invisible" worlds interlocked with one another.

(Material for this chapter was drawn from the publication, "Chalice Well-Glastonbury" a short history by F. Hardcastle, produced by the Chalice Well Trust, Little St. Michaels, Chalice Well, Glastonbury, Somerset, England)

THE WELL HEAD

JOSEPH'S TOMB

The remains of St. Joseph lay undisturbed until the year A.D. 1345. During this year, Edward III gave permission to John Bloom of London to dig for the body of Joseph, if he could first get the consent of the Abbot and the monks of Glastonbury. Permission from the Glastonbury Community was obtained and the remains of Joseph were found. A monk, R. de Boston, in the Lincolnshire Monastery, recorded: "The bodies of Joseph of Arimathea and his companions were found in Glastonbury."

The bones of Joseph were placed in a silver casket which in turn was placed in a stone sarcophagus that became the base of a shrine. This shrine was placed at the east end of the crypt under St. Mary's Chapel which caused the chapel to also be called St. Joseph's Chapel. The crypt was originally reached by a staircase going down past the ancient Norman well of St. Joseph, close to where John Bloom found the tomb of Joseph.

The silver casket could be taken from the stone sarcophagus, at will, for the benefit of the many pilgrims who came to the Abbey. Richard Pynson, in his "De Sancto Joseph ab Armathia" (A.D. 1516) narrates various miracles alleged to have been performed before the shrine. The stone altar survived the Reformation and the dissolution of the monasteries under Cromwell in A.D. 1539. Holinshed, in his "Chronicles," — A.D. 1577 (Vol. 1, pg. 40, 1807 ed.) wrote of Joseph's sarcophagus as being still in Glastonbury in his day.

John Ray, in his "itinerary" records that on June 22, 1661: "we saw Joseph of Arimathea's tomb and chapel at the end of the Church." Later, that same year, Ray returned to Glastonbury and records again seeing the sarcophagus of St. Joseph in the ruined chapel. He added that he feared the rise of another wave of Puritanical fanaticism, like that which destroyed the Holy Thorn, might desecrate the tomb of St. Joseph. Therefore, under the cloak of darkness, John Ray silently removed the altar tomb and buried it unmarked in the church yard, adjoining the east end of St. Mary's Chapel.

After being hidden for some two hundred and sixty-six years, the seemingly miraculous discovery of Joseph's Altar Tomb (Autumn of 1928) gave added validity to the Glastonbury Tradition and the British claim to the first Christian Church. It was the Rev. Lionel Smithett Lewis, M.A. (late Vicar of Glastonbury) who accidentally rediscovered the stone sarcophagus. One autumn day, while walking by the ancient cemetery, Rev. Lewis stubbed his toe on a stone object protruding from the ground, apparently lifted out of the ground by frost. Upon excavation, the stone turned out to be the long lost tomb of St. Joseph.

Today, the sarcophagus of St. Joseph rests under the Arthurian window of St. Katherine's Chapel, in St. John the Baptist Church in Glastonbury. The tomb bears the initials of Joseph of Arimathea on it — J.A., with a caduceus (the winged staff with two serpents twined about it, carried by Mercury) between them. Some researchers interpret the letters "J.A." as standing for one "John Allen." This is so recorded by Rev. Thomas Warner in his well known "History of Glastonbury." More likely, however, the name was given as a subterfuge to hide the identity of the tomb. The caduceus, the insignia of Mercury (Messenger of the gods) gives testimony that a real "messenger" of God was entombed therein. Joseph of Arimathea was just such a messenger.

TOMB OF ST. JOSEPH OF ARIMATHEA

The stone sarcophagus shows evidence of having been "wrenched" in haste from its original resting place, the work being done by some strong metal lever. The silver casket (containing the bones of St. Joseph) allegedly reposing in the tomb are missing. However, the sarcophagus contains a "plinth" or base, which would have held such a casket. A 14th century monk, Roget of Boston, recorded the tomb had an epitaph attached to it which read, in Latin: "Ad Brittanos veni post Christum Sepelivi. Docui, Quievi." (To the Britons I came after I buried the Christ. I taught, I have entered my rest.)

KING ARTHUR

One of the Traditions of Glastonbury (proudly upheld by the eleventh century A.D. monks) was that the Glastonbury Abbey was the resting place of the sepulcher of the renowned British King Arthur. Arthur's heroic deeds of valour in his battles with the pagan Saxons and Picts were sung by the Bards of old. After his last great battle with his usurping nephew, Mordred, at Camlen, in Cornwall, Arthur was dying of fatal wounds. The King asked to be conveyed to Glastonbury by water. Tennyson describes the scene; his hero speaking to his brave knight, Sir Bedivere:

"But now farewell, I am going a long way,
With these thou seest — if indeed I go
(For all my mind is clouded with a doubt) —
To the Island — valley of Avilion;
Where falls not hail, nor rain, or any snow,
Nor ever wind blows loudly; but it lies
Deep meadow'd happy, fai with orchard lawns,
And bowery hollows crown'd with summer sea,
Where I will heal me of my grievous wound,

***

So said he, and the barge with oar and sail
Moved from the brink, like some full breasted swan."

(Holy Grail, pp. 155-6)

In all western history there is no story that brings more emotional response than the legends of the fabulous King Arthur; his noble Knights of the Round Table; his great sword Excalibur and his beautiful Queen Guinevere. Arthur lived in the late 5th and early 6th centuries A.D. At that time, Britain was the scene of a bloody struggle for domination between the Britons and the invading Saxon tribes and their allies, the Picts and the Scots. What is known of Arthur is slight.

One of the earliest recorded mention of Arthur was written by Nennius, who lived about two centuries later. He wrote that Arthur fought together with the kings of Britain but that he himself was the "Dux Bellorum," meaning General or Leader. In all probability, Arthur was a great warrior, a man of immense strength and skill at waging war. Many ancient documents have been found, each reporting a series of violent battles between the Celts and the allied Saxons and Angles. Always an unnamed warrior, the leader of the Celts, was depicted as a man of unimaginable power and a great leader.

One may wonder why such an important leader was not named in so many instances. One possible reason is that the wars waged by

Arthur imposed necessary but hard taxes on the people to sustain the countries survival. Since the monks were the historians of the day, being the only ones who could write, their revenge on Arthur took the form of omitting his name from all historical records — referring to him only as a great warrior. As countless centuries rolled by, the facts of Arthur were lost in the myths and seemingly miraculous legends which, in time, diminished the credibility of the whole story. By the 19th century, many came to believe that no such person as King Arthur ever existed. Was there really such a man? Is there substance behind the fantastic exploits of the Knights of the Round Table?

The legends of King Arthur began among the Welsh bards of the seventh century. They were first printed by Caxon in A.D. 1485, in the chronicles of Sir Thomas Malory, called the "Morte d'Arthur." In more modern times, scholars began to have doubts as to the authenticity of the main facts of these legends. There are those that contend that many of the legends are altogether due to the imagination of the Welsh bards, with perhaps only the slightest of historical foundations for these stories. Some historical writers, on the other hand, acknowledge Arthur as a Romanized Briton of the 4th century, who fought to maintain Christianity against the hordes of Picts and other barbarians of the North.

Modern research has lifted the shroud of mystery from the legendary figure. Arthur emerges as an immensely dominating leader and his knights may well be figures of real personages, distorted by time and the fiction of the romancers and writers of fables. The magical sword of Arthur can be shown to have some basis in fact and the "Holy Grail" a reality. Arthur emerged as the military genius of the Britains, in A.D. 512, owing to his crushing defeat of the Saxons at the great battle of Mount Badon. This deed is found to be well documented by the chroniclers of the period.

A formal search was made for the grave of Arthur in the year A.D. 1191 by Henry de Soliaco, who was appointed Abbot of Glastonbury, after King Henry's death in 1189. Malmesbury records that King Arthur and his Queen Guinivere were buried in the monk's graveyard between two pyramids (Antiauitate, pg. 309). Matthew O. Paris also mentioned that in A.D. 1191 (pg. 138) Arthur's remains were found between two "antique pyramids."

Giraldus Cambrensis, who professes to have been an eye witness to the search, relates that at the depth of seven feet, a large flat stone was found. On the underside of the stone was fastened a lead cross. The cross was taken from the stone and on the underside, facing the stone, were the words: "Hic jacet sepultus inclytus Rex Arthurius in

Insula Avalonia." (Here lies buried in the island of Avalonia, the renowned king Arthur)

THE KING ARTHUR CROSS

The cross is lost, but a 16th century engraving suggests that it dates from before the 10th century, when St. Dunstan (Abbot of Glastonbury A.D. 936) is said to have raised the level of the cemetery. The clay terrace, which he formed, has been found and it would have buried any earlier memorial. The lead cross, most likely, was a label replacing the original stone stele which one would expect to find marking the grave of a 6th century general, such as Arthur.

Below the stone, at a depth of nine feet, was a huge coffin "of hollowed oak," which, when raised to the surface and opened was found to contain two cavities. At the head and occupying two-thirds of the space were the bones of a man of gigantic proportions with a large skull bearing ten wounds nine of which showed signs of healing. A woman's bones rested in the remaining one-third of the coffin. With her bones was a tress of yellow hair, perfect in form and color, which on being touched, fell to pieces. Arthur and Guinivere had been found at last. Their remains were first removed to a chapel in the south aisle of the Great Church and later moved to the middle of the presbytery.

In the year A.D. 1278, King Edward I and his Queen, Eleanor, kept the festival of Easter at Glastonbury. The mausoleum, containing the relics, was opened for their inspection and by their order the remains placed in separate caskets and sealed in a black marble tomb. In front of the High Altar, the skulls, of the King and Queen were to remain outside for the adoration of the people. The tomb is recorded as having survived until the dissolution of the Abbey in A.D. 1539. Remains of the tomb were found in 1931 in the western part of the choir, near the original position of the High Altar.

Excavations in 1962 and 1963 unearthed a socket which had been used as a base for a stone pillar, probably a cross. Around the socket were fragments of 16th century pottery, suggesting that the monument had been destroyed at the Reformation. Originally, the cross stood about 40 feet south of the Lady Chapel, opposite the second window from the east end. Fifteen feet further south was the wrecked remains of a small semi-underground tomb chamber of "Hypogeum." This is the type of tomb shrine to which the term "pyramid" applies. Between the cross and the tomb chamber, a large hole had been opened late in the 12th century and refilled after a very short interval. The hole went down into natural soil destroying two or three of the earliest graves, including one set close against the tomb chamber indicating it belonged to a man of power and standing. The location of the grave and the date of it having been opened leaves little doubt the burial it once contained was the one the monks identified as Arthur and Guinevere, as reported by medieval writers.

MARKER INDICATING SITE OF KING ARTHUR's TOMB

REDISCOVERED IN 1934

Not only does Glastonbury claim King Arthur's body but may also be associated with the site where Arthur is reported to have given up his famous sword Excalibur. When John Leland, King Henry III's antiquary, wandered through Somerset (about the year A.D. 1542) he found, on the River Brue, a mile from Glastonbury: "a Bridge of Stone of a 4. arches communely caullid Ponterlus, wher men fable that Arture cast in his Swerd." The bridge crosses the river between Glastonbury and the town of Street. In A.D. 1415, the river's Latin name was "Ponspericulosus". Today, rebuilt several times, it is still called "Pomparles." On John Overton's Map of Somerset (1668) it is marked as "Pomperles Bridge."

POMPARARLES BRIDGE

The question if often asked, "Why should the "Holy Grail" stories be bound up with the Arthurian legends?" The answer is not too difficult to find. Arthur was not merely a great military leader, but an avowed Christian. His Christian faith was one of the tools with which he bound Britain into unity, and with which he opposed the forces of local rivalry, local tyranny, and local ambitions. But, perhaps the strongest link is found in the pedigree of Arthur; his direct descent from Joseph of Arimathea.

The geneology of King Arthur is given by the historian John of Glastonbury. He lists Arthur as the 10th descendant from St. Joseph of

Arimathea. The following pedigree is taken from John's manuscript, giving Arthur's descent from Joseph through Arthur's mother: "Helaius, Nepos Joseph, Genuit Josus, Josue Genuit Aminadab. Aminadab Genuit Filium, qui Genuit Ygernam, de qua Rex Pen-Dragon, Genuit Nobilem et Famosum Regum Arthurum, per Quod Patet, Quod Rex Arthurus de Stirpe Joseph descendit." (Note: the original meaning of the Latin "Nepos" is not Nephew, but Grandson — White & Riddle's Latin Dictionary A.D. 1880)

If, as it can be believed, Joseph brought the Cup used at the Last Supper with him when he came to Britain, then its discovery would have been of tremendous importance. Here would be a relic, sanctified by the centuries in Britain, and by right of descent, belonging to Arthur. It could have been used as a symbol of Arthur's power to represent the Christian unity of Britain, overriding both the authority of the regional kings and the opposing forces which Arthur could barely hold in check.

In one of the earliest of the Grail literature (Grand St. Grail) we are told that after the death of St. Joseph and Josephus (his son) the keeping of the "Holy Grail" was given into the care of Alain, the son of Brons and cousin to Josephes. At Alain's death, his brother became Grail keeper, and after him six kings, the last of whom was Pelles. King Pelles, through his daughter (who married Sir Lancelot) had a grandson named Galahad, who became the special hero of the Holy Grail legends. Tradition has it that Galahad, as well as all of the knights of the Round Table, were descended from Joseph of Arimathea.

If true, the relationship between Arthur's knights and Judean Joseph would explain the curious and startling digressions concerning King David, King Solomon, and Judas Maccabees mixed in with the legends of the Arthurian Knights. In "Morte D'Arthur," which contains the "Quest of the Sangred" (Quote del St. Graal) and the "High History of the Holy Grail," scholars can trace the "Graal" stories into dim pre-Christian times, and further to the east of Palestine. The theme apparently was taken over and "Christianized" with outstanding success. However, the sage of the Graal (the pagan Cup of Plenty that became the "Sangrael," the "Sang Real," the "Chalice containing the Holy Blood, and the mysterious source of Life, Healing and Prosperity) had nothing whatsoever to do with Arthur, Joseph of Arimathea of the Christian "Chalice" — Cup of the Last Supper.

THE CUP OF THE LAST SUPPER

Many legends have grown up around the story of the Cup of the Last Supper. King Arthur and his knights bound themselves in solemn oath to find the "Holy Grail." They braved many hazards in fruitless search. Some of our most beautiful literature is written around the Quest of the "Holy Chalice." We are still intrigued with the mystery of the Cup. What was its ultimate fate? The answer may well lie in the Tradition of Glastonbury that Joseph of Arimathea had the Cup in his possession when he arrived at Avalon. He is said to have buried it within the cloaking earth of Chalice Hill, from which flows the waters of the Chalice Well.

Belief that the original Cup of the Last Supper was brought to Glastonbury and buried there has existed for over a thousand years. The strength of this belief is shown to us in the many poems, songs and stories that abound. Tennyson immortalized the tradition of the Cup coming to Glastonbury in the following verses he wrote:

"The cup, the cup, itself, from which our Lord
Drank at the last sad supper with His own.
This, from the blessed land of Aromat-
After the day of darkness, when the dead
Went wandering o'er Moriah — the good saint,
Arimathean Joseph, journeying brought
To Glastonbury, where the winter thorn
Blossoms at Christmas, mindful of our Lord.
And there awhile it bode; and if a man
Could touch or see it, he was heal'd at once,
By faith, of all his ills. But then the times
Grew to such evil that the holy cup
Was caught away to Heaven, and disappear'd.

—

To whom the monk: From our old books I know
That Joseph came of old to Glastonbury,
And there the heathen Prince, Arviragus,
Gave him an isle of march wheron to build;
And there he built with wattles from the marsh
A little lonely church in days of yore,
For so they say, these books of ours, but seem
Mute of this miracle, far as I have read.
But who first saw the holy thing today?"

While colorful and romantic stories picture the Cup of the Last Supper as a gold or silver chalice, a Passover Dish, even the Holy Grail of the Arthurian legends, one is inclined to believe the Cup was a plain drinking vessel, perhaps of wood, as was widely used in the Middle East at the time of Christ. Just such a cup exists — the "Nanteos Cup" which for over four centuries rested in the House of Nanteos, in Wales. The story of this gnarled olive wood cup starts with the destruction of the Monasteries by Henry VIII in his ruthless war against Roman Catholicism.

At the time of the destruction of the Glastonbury Abbey, Richard Whiting, the last Abbot, entrusted a wooden cup to his monks to carry away to safety. He described the cup as "the most precious treasure of our Abbey." The monks fled across the border of Wales and for awhile were safe in the remote (now ruined) Cistercian Abbey of Strata Florida. But when Henry's men entered Wales and approached the Abbey, the monks again had to flee, this time in the direction of Aberystwyth, which suggests they may have intended to escape by sea.

After some fifteen miles trudging over mountainous and marshy country, the monks arrived, travel stained and weary, at Nantous Manor, situated in a secluded valley three miles from Aberystwyth, where they sought shelter. Sympathizing with their plight, the Lord of the Manor, Mr. Powell, and his wife, extended a warm welcome and a invitation to stay and make Nanteos Manor their home. It is believed that the Prior became the family chaplain, while the elderly monks were employed in light work on the 5000 acre estate.

As the years passed, the little band of monks dwindled in numbers as one by one they passed away till only one monk remained. In the course of time, he too, lay dying in his bed when he called in the Lord of the Manor to reveal to him his secret of being custodian of the Holy Cup. After delivering the Cup into the hands of the Powells for safe keeping, he charged them that the Cup should remain at Nanteos Manor "until the church claims her own."

During the succeeding centuries, the Cup became known as the "Healing Cup" as miraculous cures were claimed by those afflicted by various sicknesses, after drinking from the Cup. A specially made glass bowl was fashioned to hold the Cup, so that chips could not be bitten from the rim by sick folks who believed that the healing water taken from the Cup would be more efficacious if a chip of the wood was consumed with it.

Often the Cup was lent out briefly for the relief of local people too sick to travel. Watches and jewelry were left as pledges against the Cup's safe return, then left permanently as thank-you offerings for recovery. Among the many written testimonies of healing is one that reads: "3rd August, 1862, The cup lent to Wm. Jones, Llanbadarn. Left a silver watch: returned 4th September, 1862. Case cured."

Another reads: "27th November 1857. Cup loaned this day to Wm. Rowlands. Ystrad, Tregaron; use of his sister ... wholly cured; left one pound. Returned 2nd January, 1858."

Letters of gratitude bear witness to more recent cases. In one, dated 1939, a clergy man vouches that two children afflicted with epilepsy drank water from the Cup and were cured within a few weeks; others tell of cures for fever, rheumatism and arthritis. As reports of these astounding cures spread over the surrounding countryside, pilgrims from all over Britain and even from overseas, began to journey to Nanteos to drink water from the famous Healing Cup.

A remarkable and more recent story is about a local Roman Catholic priest who sipped water from the Cup and was immediately cured of crippling rheumatism. Father James Wharton of St. Joseph's Church, who died in 1966 at the age of 75, is remembered by many people of the town of Upton-upon-Severn in Worchestershire, England. Father Wharton had been so crippled by rheumatism that he was unable to bend his legs at the knees. His miracle happened on August 21, 1957 — the day he journeyed 100 miles to the House of Nanteos. There, he drank from the battered wooden cup, then sank to his knees and prayed. Immediately afterward, the priest rose, his knees bending without difficulty as he walked from the room effortlessly and free from pain. Witnesses, including his housekeeper Miss Phyllis Woodward, were able to describe the remarkable transformation.

Divested of its remarkable history and miraculous cures, the Cup is not an impressive sight. Here is no silver chalice shining with spiritual light as in the stories of Malory and Tennyson, but instead, a battered piece of wood that looks more like half a coconut shell, blackened and broken. Reduced to about one-third its original size by centuries of wear. Originally, it would have measured about five inches in diameter at the top and about three inches in depth, tapering to a base, about two and a half inches across. Its edges are dented and pitted with the teeth marks of overardent pilgrims.

Are the remnants of the Nanteos Cup the remnants of the Cup used for the Sacrament at the Last Supper? Does it really have healing powers? The present owner of the Cup requires no further proof that the cup she cherishes is indeed the wonder-working Cup of the Last Supper. If she ever had any doubts, they were forever dispelled in 1959 when a ladder fell and broke the skull of her youngest daughter, Jean. The hospital reported that her case was hopeless because of severe hemorrhage. Thereupon, Mrs. Miryless took the Cup from its box and prayed. Minutes later, hospital personnel telephoned to say that the bleeding had suddenly stopped; the child would live. Jean completely recovered to become a healthy child. Coincidence? Perhaps. But in myriad and mysterious ways faith works wonders that defy scientific explanation. Whether the Cup has extraordinary healing powers or whether it was only a vehicle to motivate one's faith is a moot question. Many believe that this humble wooden vessel is the cup of the Last Supper. Who, in all sincerity, can say they are wrong?

THE NANTEOUS CUP

HOLY GRAIL = JESUS CHRIST

"And the Word was made flesh and dwelt among us (and we beheld glory, the glory of the only begotten of the Father) full of grace and truth."

"This is my body which is given for you."

"This cup is the new testament in my blood, which is shed for you."

O, three times famous Isle, where is that place that might
Be with thyself compar'd for glory and delight,
Whilst Glastonbury stood, exalted to that pride,
Whose Monastery seem'd all others to deride?
O, Who thy ruins sees, whom wonder doth not fill
With our great father's pomp, devotion, and their skill?

To whom did'st thou commit that monument to keep
That suffreth with the dead their memory to sleep,
When not great Arthur's tomb, nor hold Joseph's grave
From sacrilege had power their sacred bones to save?
He who that God-in-man to his sepulchre brought,
Or he which for the faith twelve famous battles fought.

What? Did so many Kings do honour to that place,
For avarice at last so vilely to deface?
For rev'rence to that seat which hasth ascribed been
Trees yet in Winter bloom, and bear their Summer's green.

Michael Drayton (published 1613 A.D.)

EPILOGUE

Consider the Traditions of Glastonbury. They cannot be dismissed as mere fables, for legend is not fiction, nor is truth confined only to that which can be established by documentary evidence. It is a fact that legends and traditions are generally rooted in a basis of truth. In the absence of positive proof to the contrary, there is no reason why one would not accept traditions as having a foundation in fact.

Some may dismiss all legends and traditions is the absence of clear, reliable, documentary records. However, we must remember that the whole of Britain's history (for the first 500 years of the Christian age) is almost entirely blank as regards to written records. As we have seen, such is not the case with the Traditions of Glastonbury because certain authorities have testified, in times past, to the truth of the Traditions.

Admittedly, some eminent British scholars reject the antiquity of the Traditions, holding that they were stories concocted by the Glastonbury monks to attract pilgrims and their money to Glastonbury, after the destructive fire of A.D. 1184. However, while rejecting all earlier historical references to the Traditions of Glastonbury as "later interpolations" and not supported by clear evidence, they invariably admit it is not impossible that the legends are factual.

JESUS — MARIA

Some may say the founding of the Abbey by Joseph of Arimathea and other disciples of Christ is perfectly unprovable. But, to many other minds, it is at the same time perfectly credible — its greatest probability is underwritten by uninterrupted traditions. The mystical charism of the cumulative legends and traditions of Glastonbury has, for over a thousand years, drawn pilgrims from all parts of the world. It is not without reason that William Blake (poet and mystic of the 18th century) penned his famous Glastonbury Hymn with its haunting and challenging question, never answered in the affirmative or negative:

"And did those feet in ancient time
Walk upon England's mountains green?
And was the Holy Lamb of God
On England's pleasant pastures seen?
And did the Countenance Divine
Shine forth upon our clouded hills?
And was Jerusalem builded here
Among those dark Satanic mills?

Bring me my bow of burning gold!
Bring me my arrows of desire!
Bring me my spear! O clouds unfold!
Bring me my Chariot of Fire!
I will not cease from mental fight,
Nor shall my sword sleep in my hand,
Till I have built Jerusalem
In England's green and pleasant land."

William Blake, 1757-1827

It is perfectly clear that William Blake meant to convey his belief that Jesus Christ did come to England, before He began His ministry in the Holy Land. At the age of 14, Blake became an apprentice to a London engraver and one of his engravings in those early days of his life was of Joseph of Arimathea. He shows us plainly, both as engraver and as poet, that he was aware of Christ's visit to "England's green and pleasant land," and that it had impressed him deeply.

We may never unravel all the mystery surrounding Glastonbury, but the Traditions of Glastonbury, like truth, will never die. Legend and history are inextricably mingled, making it difficult to differentiate between truth and legend in some instances. However, Glastonbury is "the holyest earthe in England" and the spirit of its Traditions is still vibrant and alive, close-knit with a living Christ.

Jesus Christ said He will return to this earth. ...

THE ISLE OF AVALON

Have you walked along the Mendips
Where His weary feet have gone,
When He climbed the Tor and looked out
O'er the Isle of Avalon?

Have you seen the Holy Thorn tree
Standing in the evening sun,
Full of blooms and scented perfume
On the Isle of Avalon?

And the lead mines on the hill-tops
I have often gazed upon,
Where He walked — a lonely figure
On the Isle of Avalon.

Up the Cheddar Gorge to Priddy,
In the rain and snow and sun,
Just to give His simple message
To the Isle of Avalon.

Near the Chalice Well His hut stood;
When the day of work was done
He would watch the golden sunset,
O'er the Isle of Avalon.

You may walk there, in His footsteps,
And your eyes will rest upon
Glastonbury's sacred mountains,
On the Isle of Avalon.

Kirsten Parsons

A PROPHECY OF MELKIN (THE BRITISH BARD)

There hath fallen on sleep.
Amid these Joseph in marble,
Of Arimathea by name,
Hath found perpetual sleep:
And he lies on a two-forked line
Next the south corner of an oratory
Fashioned of wattles
For the adorning of a mighty Virgin
By the aforesaid sphere-betokened
Dwellers in that place, thirteen in all.
For Joseph hath with him
In his sarcophagus
Two cruets, white and silver,
Filled with the blood and sweat
Of the Prophet Jesus.
When his sarcophagus
Shall be found entire, intact,
In time to come, it shall be seen
And shall be open unto all the world:
Thenceforth not water nor the dew of heaven
Shall fail the dwellers in that ancient isle.
For a long while before
The day of judgement in Josaphat
Open shall these things be
And declared to living men.

(about A.D. 1400)

This queer piece of semi-poetical prose, intended to mystify and hardly capable of translation from the Latin into English, was written by John of Glastonbury. His book this was taken from was published by Hearne in 1726 A.D.

APPENDIX A

OTHER NOTABLE BUILDINGS OF GLASTONBURY AND VICINITY

THE ABBOT'S KITCHEN

The Kitchen, belonging to the Abbot's great Guest Hall, where he entertained his visitors, was built in the early part of the 14th century. Started by Abbot Fromand (1303-22) it was completed by Abbot John de Breynton. (1333 – 41) The Kitchen is a square building with the corners cut off by the insertion of a fireplace in each and has an octagonal roof crowned by a lantern. It is a fine specimen of the 14th century style of architecture. The lantern is double, the outer octagonal, the inner circular. In the interior the roof has eight curved ribs springing from the octagon formed by the fireplace and ending at the inner lantern, leaving eight small air-holes round the central large one. This arrangement was necessary to carry off the smoke at the top of the building from the large fires that were continually kept up. Today it is used as the Abbey museum.

GLASTONBURY FROM OLD PRINT (1811)

Glastonbury town center as it looked in the early 19th century A.D. Here were held fairs and markets, often in connection with the great religious festivals. The fairs were four in number: (1) St. Dunstan's fair, on May 19th was in memory of the greatest of the abbots; (2) Holy Cross Fair was held on Sept. 14th, for there were seven fragments of the true Cross supposedly among the Abbey relics; (3) St. Michael's Fair, granted in A.D. 1127 by Henry I to the Monastery on the Tor; (4) The Fair of Our Lady, on her supposedly birthday, Sept. 8th. Only Holy Cross and St. Michael's Fairs have survived. Today, the center is marked by a Market Cross, dating from A.D. 1845 and modeled after the famous Queen Eleanor Crosses.

THE TITHE BARN AT GLASTONBURY

The Abbey barn, once known as the "Tithe Barn" is located at the corner of Bere Lane and Chilkwell Street. Built in the 14th century, it was used to store the grain due to the Abbey and consumed by the monks. As much skill has been expended in the construction of this building as in many a church. At the four corners were figures of the four Evangelists; St. Matthew on the east, St. John on the west, St. Luke on the north, and St. Mark on the south. At the end of one gable is the effigy of an Abbot. The building is in an excellent state of preservation. Inspected from the interior, it will be found to be a cruciform building, with a fine timber roof, and two large doorways in the arms of the cross. There are slits in the walls for ventilation, but no windows except a small one in each of the principal gables.

THE ALMSHOUSE AT GLASTONBURY

The Almshouse (Almonry) was a place where the alms of the Abbey were distributed to the poor of Glastonbury. To distribute these alms there was always a monk called "Almoner" (Eleemosynaris) whose business it was to make inquiry after the sick, feeble, aged, and disabled persons in the neighbourhood. At one time the old people in the almshouses received quarterly, 12s. 6d as a substitutionary grant from the Crown.

THE GEORGE OR PILGRIM'S INN

Abbot Selwood is said to be the builder of this most interesting inn. It was built in A.D. 1475 as a gift to the Chamberlain (from the Abbot) who derived his income from the hotel bills of the faithful. Up to this date, strangers were lodged at the Abbey or at the Abbot's Inn, at the Abbot's expense. So, in addition to being a gift from the Abbot, it also saved the Abbot money — as the visitors could be housed at their own expense.

The windows of George Inn appear to have been inserted at a later date. The panelled bay, the octagonal towers, (one hollow for a bell) and the whole facade are original. There is a fine hall upstairs, approached by the original staircase from below. Of the three shields over the doorway, one contains a St. George's Cross, (here at this inn the Cross was conferred on George) the center one the arms of Edward IV, and the third is left blank.

THE TRIBUNAL

This building is believed to have been the Court House of Glaston Twelve Hides, where all legal cases were heard. It was built by Abbot Beere, the last Abbot but one. Over the entrance are two panels, containing the Arms of Henry VII and the Glastonbury Rose. Nothing of interest remains in the interior except some carved oak paneling in the upper story and two ceilings.

The building has served many purposes. It was a seedman's shop, classical and commerical day-school for young gentlemen, a lawyers office, a shoe-shine shop, a vegetable market and today the Glastonbury town Museum.

ST. PATRICK'S CHAPEL DOORWAY

St. Patrick's Chapel lies within the Glastonbury Abbey grounds and was built by Abbot Beere in A.D. 1512. The date of its dedication to St. Patrick is uncertain. Over the entrance to the Chapel are the Tudor Arms; a rose with a dragon and greyhound supporters.

RUINS OF ST. MICHAEL'S CHURCH ON THE TOR

Overlooking Glastonbury is the Tor, a conical hill, standing out prominently, and forming a landmark for miles around. It is about 520 feet high and once a place of Druidic worship. When St. Patrick came to Glastonbury he found a small ruined chapel on its summit which he and his associates re-built. The original chapel may have been one built by Phaganus and Deruvianus, in the second century, A.D. During the period of Henry I there was still a church. An earthquake in A.D. 1275 destroyed all the buildings on the Tor, but Abbot John Taunton rebuilt it. The shell of his tower still stands today. The carved statues are gone but the carvings in the front wall are interesting.

Until about 1825 a fair was held at the foot of the Tor. (called Tor Fair) The charter for holding this fair was granted by Henry I, A.D. 1127, to the Abbot and monks, "To hold a fair at the Monastery of St. Michael's on the Tor, in the Island of Glastonbury." It was to last six days, five before the feast of St. Michael, and on the feast day itself. A piece of land in the place where it was held is still known as "Fair Field."

THE ABBOT'S FISH HOUSE AT MEARE

The Fish House at Meare is thought to have been a house for one of the officials of the Abbey, and as there are signs of there having been large lakes used for fish close by it was probably the residence of the person in charge of that department. It was built in the time of Abbot Adam de Sodbury. (1322-1335) The Mere (lake) was stated in 1517 to have been a mile in length and three-quarters of a mile in width. In 1939, it was recorded as being five miles in circumference and a mile and a half across. The disparity of size is likely to have arisen from measurements being taken at one time in a wet and in another at a dry season of the year. Fish was an important food for the monastery as meat was forbidden during Lent and at other times. Documents mention an annual yield of 5,000 eels from the lake at Meare.

WELLS CATHEDRAL FROM THE WELLS

The Cathedral of Wells has seen over a thousand years of English history. Tradition has it that about the year 705 A.D. King Ina founded a church here in honor of St. Andrew with a college of secular priests to serve it. When the Bishopric of Wells was founded in 909 A.D. this church became its Cathedral and these priests its canons. In the course of time the Cathedral fell into decay and was destroyed by John de Villula. A second Norman Cathedral was built in 1148 A.D. and itself vanished as completely as its predecessor.

The Cathedral we see today was begun by Bishop Reginald de Bohun about 1184-6 A.D. and his original plan was so carefully developed by later builders that the whole building forms a unity so harmonious that one is never brought up short by breaks in design or style or additions over some two and a half centuries. A striking feature of the Cathedral is the inverted arches which were added to give additional strength to the columns supporting the massive weight of the central tower.

The Wells Cathedral School founded with the See in 909 A.D. is the oldest educational foundation in Somerset. Today, after a thousand years the school continues to give its scholars not only a sound secular education, but also, what is even more precious, a Christian education.

THE GREAT SEAL OF THE GLASTONBURY ABBEY

This seal, of the time of Abbot John Chinnoch, is introduced to show the Abbey Spire. There are several other points of interest about it. The original silver seal is lost, melted no doubt, in some thieves' pot. It had two sides to it. One side has three masculine saints, Patrick, Dunstan and Benignus, with the legent, "Confirmant has res + scripti ponifices tres - the holy bishops three, assurance give to thee."

The other side of the seal has three women saints, St. Katharine with her wheel, Our Lady with the Word of God and a vase of roses in the center, and St. Margaret with her dragon. The jingle on this is "Testis adest isti, scripto pia genetrix Xti - Glastonie - God's gentle Mother dear, as witness too is here, Glastonbury."

Relics of St. Katharine were brought by Adam de Sodbury both to the Abbey and St. John's Church. St. Margaret's sandals and a bone of hers, were treasured in St. Mary's Chapel.

The architecture on the Seal is XV. Century, and gives, perhaps, some ideas of the Chapter-House, which this Abbot finished. The Seal is taken from the submission of Abbot Whiting, and all the Convent to the Oath of Supremacy.

A LEGEND OF GLASTONBURY

"Who hath not hir'd of Avalon?
Twas talk'd of much and long agon: —
The wonders of the Holy Thorn,
The which, zoon ater Christ was born,
Here a planted war by Arimathe,
Thie Joseph that com'd over sea,
And planted Christianity.
Tha za that whun a landed vust,
(Zich plazen was in God's own trust)
A stuck his staff into the groun,
And over his shoulder lookin roun,
Whativer mid his lot bevall,
He cried aloud now, 'weary all!'
The staff het budded and het grew,
And at Christmas bloom'd the whol da droo,
And still het blooms at Christmas bright,
But best tha za at dork midnight."

Written in the Somerset dialect of A.D. 1870
from oral traditions prevalent in Glastonbury

APPENDIX B

ABBOTS OF GLASTONBURY

1. — St. Patrick (A.D. 460 ?)
2. — St. Benignus (?)
3. — (Many successive Abbots whose names have been lost)
4. — Worgret (A.D. 601)
5. — Lalemund (?)
6. — Bregoretd (?)
7. — Berthwald (A.D. 670) Became Archbishop of Canterbury.
8. — Hemgesel (?) Said to have been Abbot for 25 years.
9. — Berwald (A.D. 705) King Ina, among other lands, granted this Abbot 12 hides of land at Stowey, 20 hides as Pilton, 70 hides at Wedmore, at that time an island.
10. — Albert or Albeort (A.D. 712)
11. — Echfrid or Aethfrid (A.D. 719) Founded the Great Church of the Apostles Peter and Paul. Caused a chapel to be made of gold and silver with ornaments and vessels of like precious metals which he placed in the Great Church. He also gave an altar-cloth and magnificent vestments interwoven with gold and precious stones.
12. — Cengille (A.D. 729) In the year A.D. 744 Cuthred, King of the West Saxons, confirmed by charter all former grants to the Abbey.
13. — Cumbert or Tumbert (A.D. 745)
14. — Tican (A.D. 754) He governed the Abbey six years and was buried there.
15. — Cubun (A.D. 760)
16. — Waldun (A.D. 772)
17. — Beadewlf (A.D. 794) Offa, King of the Mercians, gave this Abbot 10 hides of land for the support of his Church.
18. — Cuman (A.D. 800) In the year A.D. 802, Egbert, King of the West Saxons, gave grants of land to the Church, and for the use of the monks at Glastonbury.
19. — Mucan (A.D. 811)
20. — Cuthlac (A.D. 824)
21. — Ealmund (A.D. 851)
22. — Hereferth (A.D. 857) Earl Ethelbald gave this Abbot a grant of land for the Old Church of the Mother of God, Mary, and for the use of the monks of the monastery at Glastonbury. King Alfred gave to the Abbey a piece of the wood of our Saviour's cross, which Pope Martin had given him.

23. — Styward (A.D. 891) He is said to have scourged his monks. Pictures of him always show him with a scourge or broom in his hand.

24. — Aldhunus or Athelmus (A.D. 905) Said to be the uncle to Dunstan. He was the first Bishop of Wells; afterwards, Archbishop of Canterbury.

25. — Alfric or Elfric (?)

26. — Dunstan (A.D. 941) Received many gifts from different kings under which he lived. King Edmund gave a charter to the monastery written in letters of gold, in a book of Gospels; he also bequeathed his body to the monastery when he died. Dunstan laid the foundations of the Great Church and a set of monastic offices.

27. — Elsius (A.D. 956) Known as the 'usurping' Abbot. He was appointed by King Edwy when he had banished Abbot Dunstan.

28. — Egelward or Aelwardus (A.D. 962) King Edgar gave him several grants including 56 hides of land in various places.

29. — Elfstan (?)

30. — Sigebar or Sicgarus (A.D. 965) Received great grants of land from King Edgar, including vestments, a cross of gold and silver for the high altar, a silver shrine covered with gold and ivory images and a number of relics. Sigebar was appointed Bishop of Wells A.D. 975.

31. — Beorthred or Brichredo (A.D. 1000)

32. — Brithwin (?) Appointed Bishop of Wells A.D. 1027.

33. — Egelward (A.D. 1027)

34. — Egelnoth (A.D. 1053) Was deposed of his Abbotship at the time of the Norman Conquest.

35. — Thurstinus or Thurstan (A.D. 1082) Rebuilt the Great Church Major Ecclesia and the Vetusta Ecclesia.

36. — Herlewinus (A.D. 1101) Pulled down Thurstan's works and started rebuilding.

37. — Sigfrid (?) Appointed Bishop of Chichester.

38. — Henry of Blois (A.D. 1126) Appointed Bishop of Winchester A.D. 1134 but retained appointment of Abbey of Glastonbury for 45 years. He rebuilt the monastery from the foundations, a bell-tower, a chapter-house, cloister, lavatory, refectory, dormitory, and infirmary with a Chapel, splendid large palace, an exterior, gateway of squared stones, large brew-house and stabling for many horses, and many ornaments for the Church.

39. — Robert (?) Prior of Winchester. Built a Chapel and a Chamber.

40. — (Peter Marci, a monk, managed the Abbey under King Henry

II) The monastery was destroyed by fire on May 24, 1184. Rebuilding started immediately.

41. — Henry de Soliaco (A.D. 1189) During his appointment King Arthur's bones were discovered.

42. — Savaric (A.D. 1192) The Church was in disrepair. His appeals to Rome for help in rebuilding ignored. Abbey involved in wrangles and disputed.

43. — William Pica (?) Died in Rome under suspicion of having been poisoned.

44. — William Vigor (A.D. 1219) Settled quarrels between monks of Glastonbury and the Bishops of Wells and Bath.

45. — Robert Prior (A.D. 1233) Chosen Abbot against the wishes of the monks, voluntarily resigned in A.D. 1234.

46. — Michael of Ambresbury (A.D. 1234) Erected many monastic buildings and continued work of the Choir and Transepts of the Great Church. Left the monastery clear of debt and the land well tilled. Resigned on account of his age in A.D. 1252.

47. — Roger Forde (A.D. 1252) A native of Glastonbury and noted for literary attainment and famous eloquence.

48. — Robert Pederton or Petherton (A.D. 1261)

49. — John Taunton (A.D. 1274) Built many noble structures. Gave many books to the library and costly vestments to the Church. In A.D. 1278, King Edward I and Queen Eleanor, kept Easter at Glastonbury.

50. — John de Kancia (Cantia) or Kent (A.D. 1291) Bestowed many rich vessels and vestments upon the Church of Glastonbury. He also furnished the completed Choir and its Altars.

51. — Geffry Fromont or Fromond (A.D. 1303) Caused the Great Church to be dedicated after the Central Tower was completed and the Eastern part of the Nave vaulted. He also began the Great Hall of the Monastery. The Abbey Barn was probably erected.

52. — Walter Taunton (A.D. 1322) Caused the great Choir Screen to be built. Gave many costly ornaments and vestments to the Church, Added books to the library.

53. — Adam de Sodbury (A.D. 1323) Completed the vaulting of the Nave, united the Galilee to St. Mary's Chapel, built the Altar of St. Silvester and St. George. He set up the Abbey Clock and Bells and the great Organ.

54. — John Brienkton or Breynton (A.D. 1334 or 1335) Completed the Great Hall with kitchen and other offices. Began the Abbot's Chapel and made many other improvements.

55. — Walter Monington or de Maynton (A.D. 1341) Lengthened the Choir by two bays and refaced its interior. Built the Retro-

choir and vaulted the whole of his work.

56. — John Chinnock (A.D. 1374) Completed the Chapter House and rebuilt the Cloisters. Finished work begun by his predecessors and erected the Dormitory and Fratry.

57. — Nicholas Frome (A.D. 1420) Probably built the Abbot's Kitchen although some authorities credit the work to his predecessor.

58. — Walter More (A.D. 1456) Died the year of his election.

59. — John Selwood (A.D. 1456)

60. — Richard Beere (A.D. 1493) Sent to Rome by King Henry VII as Ambassador. He built the greater part of the Edgar Chapel. Erected the vaulting beneath the central Tower and probably added the Tower itself, causing a partial collapse. He remedied this by inserting "St. Andrew's Arches" under each Transept Arch, as at Wells. He then added Flying buttresses to the East end of the Choir and built the Lorettor Chapel. He excavated and built the Crypt under the Galilee (Porch) and Chapel of St. Mary. He built a Chapel of the Holy Sepulchre at the South end of the Nave. Also, the Almshouses and Chapel on North side of Church, the Manor House of Sharpham, and new apartments in the Monastery for priests and for Royal Guests.

61. — Richard Whiting (A.D. 1524) Completed the Edgar Chapel and made many improvements in the Abbey. In A.D. 1539, at the "Dissolution" of the Monasteries — he was found guilty of treason and was excecuted.

AN OLD GLASTONBURY COLLECT

Almighty, everlasting God, Who didst entrust Thy most blessed servant, Joseph, to take down the lifeless body of Thine Only — Begotten Son from the Cross, and to perform the due offices of humanity, hasten, we pray Thee, that we, who devotedly recall His memory, may feel the help of Thine accustomed pity, through the same, Our Lord. Amen (Translated)

ISLE OF AVALON

Avalon's island, with avidity
Claiming the death of pagans,
More than all in the world beside,
For the entombment of them all,
Honoured by chanting spheres of prophecy:
And for all time to come
Adorned shall it be
Abbadare, mighty in Saphat,
Noblest of pagans,
With countless thousands

INDEX

C

D

E

F

N

O

P

Q

R

S

T

U

Pictorial Views
of
GLASTONBURY TRADITIONS

Color Photography by **DEREK R. M. BRAY**, M.B.K.S.

The Somerset County Town of Glastonbury

The cradle of English Christianity where an infant church was planted by those who personally knew our Lord.

Glastonbury's Special Commemoration Ceremony

The church of England holds annual ceremonies of re-dedication to Christ in the Lady Chapel at the Abbey.

The Abbey Church

Looking west through the eastern part, completed in 1213. The nave and west end seen in the distance was added before 1250.

The Lady Chapel

The Lady Chapel also known as St. Joseph's Chapel has wide expanses of fine ashlar masonry in cream-colored Doulting stone enriched with geometrical patterns with foliage and tendrils.

South Side of the Lady Chapel

The Lady Chapel was the first rebuilding after the disastrous fire of 1184. It was built in the Romanesque style of the twelfth century and replaced the venerable Old Church of St. Mary.

South Side of Lady Chapel

Tradition has that the Virgin Mary was buried beneath the burial place of Joseph of Arimathea. Could this be the 'secret of the Lord?'

Jesus - Maria

Believed to be an ancient piece of masonry preserved from the fire of 1184. Perhaps to register the site of 'Our Lady's Dowry'.

North Door of the Lady Chapel

The doorway is part of the original design but the magnificent sculptures were completed a generation later.

Interior of the Lady Chapel looking west whose dimensions significantly match those of the Wilderness Tabernacle.

Glastonbury Abbey Cross

A gift of Queen Elizabeth II to mark the site of this Christian monument.

Cross Inscription

"The Cross, the symbol of our faith, the gift of Queen Elizabeth II, marks a Christian sanctuary so ancient that only legend can record its origin."

Wyrrall, or Weary All Hill

Where Joseph and his companions first landed on the Isle of Avalon – now Glastonbury.

Descendant of Original Holy Thorn Tree

It, as all other budded from it, keeps the habit of blooming both in December and again in May.

Glastonbury Holy Thorn Tree

One of several in the Abbey grounds budded from the original thorn tree. St. Patrick's Chapel in the background.

Blossoms of the Holy Thorn Tree

(Crataegus Monogyna Praecox)

The Glastonbury Abbey Kitchen

The Abbey kitchen built in the 14th century by Abbot Breynton remains roofed and complete with four walls and has four immense chimneys in the corners of the interior.

Chalice Well Garden

At the foot of Chalice Hill is a well, encompassed by a beautiful garden where a fountain has been constructed so visitors may drink the waters of the well.

Chalice Well Lid

Patterned after a 13th century design symbolizing the Bleeding Lance and the visible and invisible World's interlocked with one another.

Window in Parish Church in Bath

Commemorating the arrival of St. Joseph to Britain, who is holding his famous staff which is bursting into blossoms as he thrusts it in the fertile soil of Glastonbury.

Window in Parish Church in Bath

St. Joseph accompanied by his followers, some of whom are women, as he meets King Arviragus.

Sarcophagus of St. Joseph

The sarcophagus of St. Joseph resting under the Arthurian window of St. Katherine's Chapel in St. John the Baptist Church in Glastonbury.

The Lead Cross

"To the Britons I came after I buried the Christ. I taught, I have entered my rest."

St. John's Church

In the north transept of St. John the Baptist Church in Glastonbury can be seen the sarcophagus of St. Joseph of Arimathea, found in 1928.

The Priddy Church

The Parish Church of Priddy say: "As sure as our Lord was at Priddy" and a carol sung by the children begins; "Joseph was a metal merchant".

The Pilton Church

The Parish Church of Pilton is the home of the famous banner portraying Jesus as a young boy in a boat, accompanied by Joseph of Arimathea.

Place Manor Church

Place Manor in St. Anthony-in-Roseland has traditional ties to Joseph, the boy Jesus, and the Cornish tin mines.

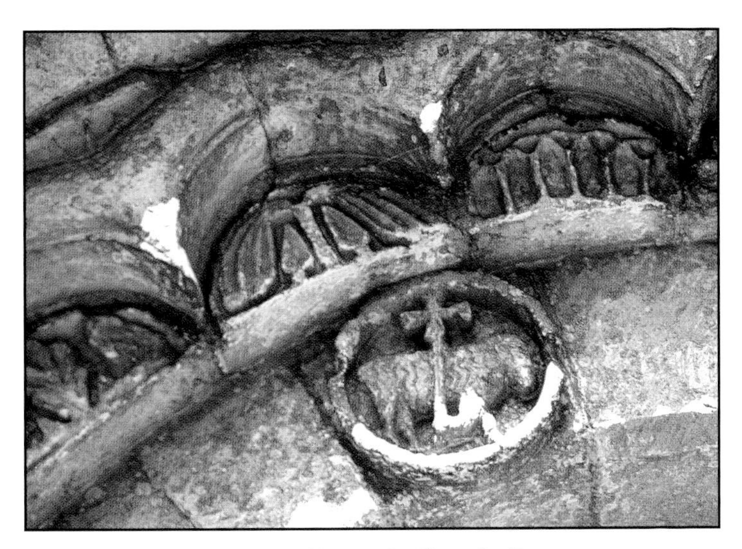

Place Manor Church South Doorway

The 1000 year old carvings over the door display an anchor, and a lamb and Cross insignia, a symbol of Jesus Christ.

The 'Ealde Churche'

After the death of Mary, her home was covered over by a wattle building patterned after the Wilderness Tabernacle, and became known as the 'Ealde Churche'. Later a stone church was built over it.

The 'Ealde Churche'

Later a lead roof was added for protection. In time the church became known as the 'Culdee Church' or 'Church of the Refugees' a title that adhered to the early British Church for centuries.

St. Michael's Mount

St. Michael's Mount off the coast of Marazion in Cornwall is the 'Ictis' island once the center of the metal trade between Phoenicia and Britain.

Phoenician Traders

Herodotus, writing in the 5th century B.C., describes the Phoenicians bargaining for the tin from Britain, known to them as the Cassiterides, or Tin Isles.

A Tunic Cross

They are made of local stone with a crudely cut Christian cross on one side and on the other side the figure of a young boy wearing a knee length tunic.

A Tunic Cross

These crosses may well portray an age-old memory of the visits of the young Jesus to Britain in the company of his uncle Joseph of Arimathea.

Meare Lake Village

A reconstruction of a lake village excavated near Glastonbury dating from the time of Christ.

Reconstructed Hut

An actual reconstruction of one of the excavated wattle huts plastered over.

The George Inn

The George or Pilgrim's Inn built in 1475 was where wealthy guests to the Abbey were housed. Today it is a private hotel and inn.

The George Inn

Over the doorway can be seen three shields. The left one contains the St. George Cross and the center one the Arms of Edward IV. It is recorded that the Cross was confered on St. George in this building.

The Tribunal

Court House of Glaston Twelve Hides, where all the law courts were held. Today it is the Glastonbury town museum.

Arviragus

Stained glass window in St. John's Church of King Arviragus of the Silurian dynasty of Britain and cousin of the British warrior Caradoc whom the Romans renamed 'Caractacus'.

Joseph of Arimathea

Stained glass window in St. John's Church commemorating Joseph of Arimathea coming to Britain.

Joseph of Arimathea arriving in Somerset

King Arviragus receiving Joseph and his twelve companions, and listening to the message of Christ, bestowed upon the little band of refugees twelve hides of land for a Christian community.